C000184849

Contents

Introduction

"Let me show you how easy it is to make big money from home in just a few hours a day using the magic of eBay!"

Welcome to *eBay Confidential* where you'll learn to make big profits on eBay, starting today. Running an eBay business is quite unlike any other opportunity we've seen so far, it's enjoyable, easy to run, very profitable. It suits almost every lifestyle, whether you view this as a part time opportunity, or you want to join us as full-time eBay PowerSellers.

And it doesn't matter what you are selling, be it handbags or jewellery, kiddies' clothing or designer dresses, rare antiques and collectibles, or almost any product you care to name, **you CAN make money on eBay**.

eBay Confidential is all you ever need to share in the massive profits being made by countless other people, all over the globe, in all walks of life, in all areas of commerce and industry.

Let my experience be your guide. But first, take a look at what's inside your special bumper issue of *eBay Confidential* and share other exclusive ideas we have to help your business grow quickly and prosper. Today we'll talk you through the simple but very important start up procedure, and we'll help you decide what to sell, whether you choose products yourself or copy our suggestions. You'll see how to describe your goods to tempt multiple bidders and high end results.

It's one of the easiest businesses ever to begin and operate and you are going to love what's in store for you because:

- **You Really Can Wake Up £100 Better Off!** No two days are ever the same on eBay, there's always some new experience awaiting you. That item you listed at £2 for example, you thought might go unsold, attracts multiple bidders in the last thirty minutes of the sale and ends up fetching triple figures, even while you were asleep. Bear in mind, while you sleep, in other countries people are wide awake and searching for items just like those you are selling. It's not unusual to wake up £100 or more better off than when you went to bed the night before. This morning I woke up to find three of five test prints I listed the other day already have £5 bids. Not so great in itself, but hugely exciting when you consider those three prints came from an 1874 bound volume of *Illustrated London News* from which hundreds more prints are still to upload.

- **Two Ping Pong Postcards sold for £215!** Nothing quite beats the thrill of last minute bidding on your auctions bringing prices way beyond your wildest expectations. For instance, a short while ago I listed two postcards, artist drawn, from about 1902, on the subject of ping pong which meant little or nothing to me at the time. My starting price of £4.99 attracted one or two bids and stood at £9.99 until the day before the auction ended. On the morning of the sale I discovered the price had risen to £75.00! That's where it stayed until about five minutes before the end when I switched off expecting little to change. An hour later I discovered the cards went for £215 as a result of frantic last minute bidding between a major ping pong enthusiast in Las Vegas and the International Table Tennis Museum in the Swiss Alps where the cards now have a beautiful new home. Now I know ping pong – table tennis – is a popular niche collecting area on eBay, something I'll bear firmly in mind at buying expeditions at flea markets and auctions.

- **It's An Automatic Money-spinner!** With a little practice and experience you really can predict almost exactly how much you will earn this week and next week, and how much time and effort is needed. List a few items more, work just a few hours longer, have more in your bank account at the end of the week. It isn't work, not in the real sense of the word, eBay is more a way of life, it's enjoyable, and *can be* hugely profitable, too.

When you see how easy it is to make money, you'll be hooked, and eager for more trade tips and insider secrets from *eBay Confidential* to help you make more money next month, and the month after that.

Our promise to you is total coverage of everything you need to know to earn a good or a great living on eBay, from sourcing products to taking money from your new customers, fulfilling orders, and generating great feedback to tempt even more people to buy from you.

It isn't complicated, and you can begin selling today and make money to grow a business as big as you want it to be.

But I can't tell you everything today. There's a lot to cover, a lot to learn, and you must keep on learning to enjoy the biggest rewards.

Trying to learn everything in one go would make your head spin and you'd probably end up confused and daunted.

My sole concern now is getting you up and running and enjoying your first taste of the incredible fun (and profits) waiting for you on eBay. Remember this is just the beginning because every month I'm going to be sending you more and more tips to help your profits skyrocket.

Special Bonus – members-only *eBay Confidential* website!

But you won't have to wait weeks – or even days – for information gleaned exclusively for our readers. I want you to profit fast from new ideas and selling trends before anyone beats you to them. So as part of our package you'll find hot new information posted on our members-only web site, all you have to do is log in and collect it.

Some subjects, such as recommended wholesale suppliers and dropshipping companies, will be covered in depth for our readers and kept well away from search engines, and others not authorised to view. Every issue of *eBay Confidential* shows you how to access these comprehensive eBay Selling reports, industry trends, hot product news, and there's even a special section to help you cash in fast on big spend seasons like Christmas, Valentine's Day, Halloween.

I didn't mention the web site in my first letter to you because I wanted it to be a surprise and because I have a reputation for under-promising and over-fulfilling that extends to most areas of my live, even on eBay. I'll tell you all about that on the web site and in monthly bulletins.

If you're new to business you could make more money than you ever thought possible. If you're already in business you'll find lots of new ideas for selling more and more of your products (and others we'll recommend to you each issue), and you'll see how to expand your business worldwide while working even fewer hours than you're working right now.

To be honest, I really think you are going to love what I have planned for you. I've put in lots of information, masses of time-sensitive advice, some great freebies too. I've written most of this myself and obtained other articles and reports from some of the world's most experienced eBay experts. I'm not charging anything extra for these bonus items, they're yours free, just go to www.1st-in-auctions.com for a tiny taste of what's to come.

So what now? Well, I suggest you make yourself a cup of tea and read through this special bumper issue right away, read it several times if you like, visit the web site, ask me a question online – I'll do my best to answer right away, certainly within twenty four hours.

And once you've done all that, don't wait another second, turn on your computer, register on eBay, make this the day you join me and countless other people making a great living on eBay and enjoying every minute of it.

And what do I want from you in return? Nothing much, I'd like you to enjoy and benefit from information I'm sourcing just for you, and I'd like to know that once you start making money on eBay you let me know about it, because I'd like to think the next eBay success story I read will be yours!

Best wishes

Avril Harper
Platinum PowerSeller and editor of
eBay Confidential

Getting Started

How to start your £1,000+ a week eBay empire!

Imagine this: Monday morning instead of going out to work, you sit down, switch on your computer, and you decide exactly how many hours you'll work this week and how much money you'll make.

If you want a day off you can have one; if the dog has a vet's appointment today you can go with him; if the kids need new shoes there's something else you can handle yourself. No need ever to ask permission for time off, no having to work when you're ill, and if you want to work nights while others work days that your decision, too.

That's what life is like for most full-time eBay sellers, and lots of part-timers, too. And it's the most exciting and exhilarating home business ever, as millions of people already know.

Fortune magazine says more than 48 million active sellers 'selected, priced, bought, sold and shipped about $32 billion worth of merchandise in 2004', a figure that's growing daily. Many great case studies exist, such as Trevor George, from Scunthorpe, ID 'british-jurassic-fossils', who sold more than 5,000 fossils on eBay last year at up to £2,200 a time (revealed in the *Sunday Times* 20ᵗʰ February 2005), and a West Virginia couple the *Wall Street Journal* says average $600,000 a month on eBay.

The *Sunday Times* revealed numerous people in the UK making a fantastic living from home, some using eBay as their sole marketing platform, others as part of a wider trading schedule.

They include:

• Julie King – killer-heels-com – from North Tyneside, who sells shoes and boots and expects to turn over £150,000 this year, up from last year's £98,000.

• Helen Southcott and Matthew Ogborne from Bristol – MoggieX – who sell digital cameras, DVD players and other consumer electronics.

They reckon one million pound plus turnover is just a few months away.

There's a lot of money to make, a lot of selling taking place under one roof and a great business for you to start today. There's nothing difficult involved and no high set-up costs to worry about, no special skills or experience are needed.

What you do need is:

• A Computer.
• Internet Access, preferably with Broadband.
• A Digital Camera or Scanner, nothing expensive, and you could do without by using pictures from product owners.
• A Credit Card, to open an eBay account, not necessarily for making payments.
• An eBay Sellers' Account.
• A PayPal Account, not essential but highly advantageous, especially when you begin selling worldwide using PayPal to convert currencies, saving you lots of time and trouble and hefty bank conversion fees. Go to www.paypal.com and follow the simple sign up process.
• Something to Sell, preferably lots of items to sell.
• Time, Energy, Determination, Commitment.

Money? You don't need a lot and you could start by selling surplus personal possessions with as little as 15p to promote your item on eBay, from which you plough proceeds back into sourcing and listing more items.

I can honestly say I never invested one penny of my own into starting my eBay business which now generates a minimum £1,000 a week.

I began by selling a handful of duplicate vintage postcards from my own collection, taking payment through PayPal, also paying eBay fees through PayPal, and using surplus money to increase my stock. The stock expanded, the business grew, and I have never looked back.

The same goes for people like Stephen Rose of Indianapolis who now runs college courses showing others how to make money on eBay. "In many ways it's like a gold rush", he says, "and the beauty of it is, there's an opportunity for people to make money and not work for anyone else, not even leave their house."

So what are these millions of people selling, which are the best sellers, where is your place in the overall picture?

At any time eBay lists dozens of main categories on its Home Pages, some containing hundreds of sub-categories with often thousands of different products being auctioned. Today they include a pair of boots said to be haunted and the chance to become sole beneficiary of a young man's will. Alongside you'll find CDs, books and audio cassettes (the choice of the biggest PowerSellers generating 12,000 plus sales each month) and old postcards (a UK man sells 2 to 3 thousand cards a month – you'll read about him later), and much more besides.

So where do you get those items?

Locating items to sell is the fun part, it's exciting, enjoyable, and you can even turn a day out with the family into a moneymaking experience. My daughters and I, we're all eBayers, (two of us PowerSellers,) buy mainly at boot sales and flea markets, collectors' fairs and trade shows. Not only do we get to find new items to sell, often at fantastic mark-ups, we also get to enjoy a day out together, having lunch somewhere nice, sometimes shopping for personal goods. The best thing is, no matter what we spend on ourselves, we're always quids in when we've sold our stock items on eBay.

Having products to sell is the most important part of running your business and an area we'll pay very special attention to in *eBay Confidential*. We'll take you on the whole gamut of buying at auction, liquidation sales, boot sales and flea markets, where bargains are plentiful and a little inside knowledge can lead to the most spectacular discoveries.

Like a bundle of old newspapers I bought for £1 at a local weekly flea market, initially to sell in bulk for a few pounds more, which I later decided to list individually and made £5 each on twenty newspapers and £20 to £30 on the remaining four. Well over £100 pure profit for less than an hour's work.

We'll also show you hundreds of products and places to find items generating the kind of profits my

family and I and countless others sell on eBay each week. You'll learn how to pick up items for pennies, how to describe them for fast profit and enjoy the experience of making big money for items that cost you little or nothing.

We buy pieces of vintage jewellery – bracelets, pendants, tie pins – in big bundles at auction, often paying a fiver or less for a plastic bag containing twenty or more items. Cleaned up, a box added, a great picture taken of the product, and suddenly something that cost us so little has people bidding ten, twenty, thirty pounds a time. Sometimes more. It's so very, very easy and anyone can replicate our experience as you will discover from countless examples and case studies found only in *eBay Confidential*.

These are other ways we'll show you to obtain stock, such as:

- **Items you make yourself**, such as craftwork goods, books you've written or adapted from public domain titles, etc. Don't worry, you don't need artistic or writing skills, we'll show you how to create high-demand products from basic materials, and how to create your very own unique best-selling books (also prints, photographs, artworks) from artistic works created by experts long ago which are now out of copyright and yours for the asking.

- **Items you've found at boot sales, auction, flea markets, jumble sales, auction, liquidation sales.** Easy, very easy, and we'll let you in on hundreds of ways to get the best items with the highest profit margins for the lowest possible prices.

- **Things you've bought for personal use and no longer want.** Take a look in your attic, the garage, spare bedroom, ask relatives for unwanted items, chances are you'll find dozens, more likely hundreds of different things you no longer want but other people are willing to pay high prices to own. But how do you list those items on eBay, what words best describe your castoffs, how much should you ask, do you sell locally or worldwide? We'll answer those questions for you in *eBay Confidential* or via our subscriber only web site.

- **Items you've bought retail or wholesale with intention to sell on eBay.** One of the best places to buy, and also one of the worst. We'll show you how to locate genuine wholesale companies. eBay sellers and dropship companies, and ensure you never fall foul of scamsters keen to take your money for second class goods, even no goods at all.

- **Items normally sold in your own or another person's other business activity.** If you're already in business and not selling on eBay, you'll kick yourself for not discovering sooner how profits can be doubled, even tripled, or more, from a few simple eBay listings. You'll find overheads lower than before, customers more plentiful, work less intense and, best of all, you'll be selling 24 hours a day, all over the world, without ever being physically present.

- **Dropship Sources.** This is where you sell items belonging to others who agree to ship the item directly to your customers. Typically you pay a fixed fee agreed in advance, preferably to firms selling continuous lines of quality, high demand goods, such as designer clothing, jewellery, remaindered books, as opposed to one-off items like antiques and collectibles.

- **Items Bought on eBay which you consider might fetch higher prices with better descriptions or in alternative categories,** and so on. We'll share a simple trick for ensuring you change just one word in another person's product description to ensure one hundred per cent or more profits on everything you buy.

- **Commission Selling**, as where you sell other people's goods for a fixed share of the proceeds, sometimes with you paying listing fees, more often the vendor pays. A business that's generating multi-million dollar turnovers in America and is largely unknown in Britain, we'll give precise details for starting your own commission selling base, with all the contact details, advertising materials, sample agreement forms, you'll ever need. You'll also learn how to pick and choose products offering the highest commissions from people who'll pay all the advertising costs even in the unlikely event their product doesn't sell.

Getting started on eBay right now

Ok, let's get to work! To register, go to www.ebay.co.uk and at the very top of the page click on 'register'. This will take you to another page where you'll give information about yourself and choose a name (eBay ID) by which you'll be known on eBay. You'll also choose a password that allows you and only you to access your personal buying and selling pages on eBay.

When that's done, eBay sends you an acknowledgement email which you must confirm as correct or requiring amendment. Then you're ready to begin buying and selling. Selling is very easy and only when you list your first item for sale will eBay request credit card details, both to prove you are genuine and a serious trader, as well as to pay for your advertising on eBay. There are other ways to pay, including PayPal, cheque, direct debit, whatever suits you best.

Spend as long as possible studying what other people are selling, choose role models, check how many items they sell each month. Do this by clicking into one of their listings, click on feedback comments, notice how much feedback they have received in the past month, six months, one year. Not every buyer or seller leaves feedback so these numbers will be on the low side. When you find someone selling several thousand items a month of products you'd like to sell, this is a possible role model for you. Notice how they describe their products, which categories they use, but don't copy too closely or you risk breaking copyright laws. Emulate, don't copy too closely.

If you feel confident, try listing something for sale. It's easy, more so if you use the simple step-by-step quick start we've provided just for our subscribers at: www.1st-in-auctions.com/QuickStart.html

Why you should choose your eBay name carefully

Aim for a memorable descriptive ID especially if you intend a full time business on eBay. It looks more professional and people are more likely to remember and buy from you again later. Very few people remember to 'Save to Favourite Sellers'.

Make your ID sensible, not silly. I sell paper collectibles under the ID toppco. Toppco stands for 'The Original Printed Paper Company' which is also the name for my eBay shop and the url for my offline site, still to be designed, www.toppco.com

eBay – just another numbers game – how to play it to win – the never-ending story!

As I never tire of saying: I view all business as a numbers game, and eBay the most enjoyable of all.

If you set out to succeed the numbers will always work in your favour. But it's one thing listing hour after hour, day after day, working hard, never taking time off – and quite another to make a few simple changes in your business that can quite easily double your profits almost immediately.

This is what to do:

• Get more new customers.
• Increase the average spend per customer.
• Turn one time buyers into regular buyers and make them your selling priority.

To explain how this works we've uploaded a great article by marketing legend Bob Leduc who gives much useful advice to our readers. (www.1st-in-auctions.com/Leduc.html).

Leduc says:

> *"You'll be amazed at the impact a small increase in each category can have on your total volume of business. Do you think you can increase each of these 3 categories by just 5% or 10% – or maybe more? An increase of only 10% in each category will increase your total income by 33%. A 25% increase will almost double it.'*

Back to basics and think how much more you could make if you:

• Sell your items for 5% more.
• Get 5% more people to buy from you again.
• Get 5% more people to buy more than one product from you at a time.
• Reduce your operating costs by 5%.
• Upload 5% more items.
• Attract 5% more visitors and buyers.

• Sell 5% more items outside of eBay.
• Contact past buyers and enquirers 5% more times each month.
• Send out 5% more newsletters

...I could go on much longer, the numbers will always work in my favour, so let's look at ways to put these ideas into practice, starting this issue with aiming to earn 5% more profit from your listings.

Sell your items for 5% more

This is easy and best achieved by studying other people selling products similar to those you are selling, only more successfully.

Look at their listings, ask yourself:

• **What was their starting price?** Opinion differs over starting price, the general view being that a very low starting price generates early bids and costs less, while high starting levels mean you won't sell at a pittance. There is no easy answer, you must check what suits you best. For my part I find low starting prices attract multiple bidders and a possible bidding frenzy in the final few hours. Not to mention lots of second chance offers. I like low starting prices but know I'll come a cropper sometimes and sell at far less than the product cost me.

• **How do they describe their items?** Is your listing packed with spelling and typing mistakes while theirs is well laid out, word perfect, a pleasure to read? If the product itself is spelled incorrectly no one will find it.

• **Which category did they use?** Very often a change of category brings unexpected improvements. For example, last week my daughter and I bought 120 pairs of dog breed cufflinks, 60 breeds each. We weren't sure where to list: under cufflinks or dog breeds. I chose 'Jewellery and Watches>men's jewellery>cufflinks; she went for individual dog breeds under 'Collectibles>animals>dogs>specific breed'. Seven days later, she sold one pair, I sold eleven. We'll try all under 'cufflinks' this week and maybe once more under 'dogs' just to be sure it wasn't a fluke.

• **Do they list benefits while you list features?** Features tell what the product looks like, how it is made, who made it, how much it costs? Benefits are what your product does for customers, how it improves their appearance, how it saves time and money, how it makes life more enjoyable. Benefits are what sell, not just features. List the benefits of your product and list, list, list them.

• **How does their listing differ from yours**, in how many ways, to what extent?

Bear in mind you are not trying to change everything about your auction; you're looking for 5% better results. Change everything and you could actually cut profits and you'll never know which was the real factor influencing their better results.

Do controlled testing, changing just one element of each listing compared to others getting better results, until you find exactly what the main difference is that makes them more successful.

Once you achieve optimum, continue testing for better results, what's good today might be a whole lot better tomorrow.

Spend a little time looking for people successfully listing the type of things you'd like to sell, then study them very carefully, let them by your coach,

Product Sourcing

WHAT SELLS ON EBAY? How to let eBay help you find best-selling products

Several ways exist to determine best selling products, most important of which are:

• **eBay produces a regular 'Hot Items' report**, based mainly on USA figures (ebay.com) which we've found works just as well for our UK sales. Download your pdf copy at: http://pages.ebay.com/sellercentral/whatshot.html

• **Every so often eBay's home page lists the top ten (sometimes more) best selling items.** Click through quickly for details as eBay promotions change quickly, even in minutes, and it may be some time before a specific list reappears.

• **Inside each selling category eBay lists the hottest items and most frequent search terms**. Go to any eBay Home Page, go to the Categories link down the left side, click on one and scroll down the page. At the left you'll see popular search terms where you can click through to see which items are attracting higher and multiple bids. Record these words to use as keywords in your listings. But check for changes in keywords and apply them sparingly or risk accusations of 'keyword spamming' and a warning from eBay.

• **Go to http://pulse.ebay.co.uk (or .com)** where several great product research ideas present themselves. At the left you'll see the most popular search terms overall on eBay. Now go to the search box, left side, above the search terms, and choose a category. Wait for the page to change and again you'll see the most popular search terms within that category. Go again to the search box and click on the menu to locate numerous sub-categories within your chosen main category. Click through and discover even tighter, more closely approximately niche market search terms. For 'niche' read 'perfect marketing strategy!'

- **Now scroll right down to the bottom of the page** where you'll find the current most visited listings, some with thousands of impressions and hundreds of bids. Stay awhile, study those high visit items, they are the kind you should aim for.

- **At the Pulse site you'll see up to ten eBay sellers listed**, based on highest number of items in shops and auctions for your chosen category. Click on the shop names (the top line of emboldened text, see what's being sold in such huge quantities). While inside those sellers' pages, go to the right of the screen where it says 'Sort By', click on the arrow and choose 'Price: highest first'. Now feast on a multitude of products that are working well for eBay's most successful sellers.

- **Following on from the last tip**, it's one thing learning what is selling today, but quite another knowing which of those items are regular sellers and what prices they fetch. Get details by clicking on 'Advanced Search', top right on any eBay site and wait for the page to change. Type key words, such as 'silver charms' into the search box where you can also choose a category but I prefer not to. Now tick the 'Completed Listings Only' box and then 'Search'. The results will be auctions that ended for products based on your chosen terms. Go to the 'Sort By' box and choose 'Price: Highest First'. They're the products to go for. See the next tip.

- **You can even see how many sales have been made of similar or related items by individual sellers**. Go to 'Advanced Search' again, click through, and this time choose 'Items by Seller' at the left, wait for the page to change, then enter the seller's ID and tick 'Include Completed Listings'. Next page is a real eye-opener, a marketer's dream come true, a chance for you to learn exactly what others have sold, how much they made per listing, even how many bids were placed, and how many second chance offers were made from one listing. There's a lot of information on this page and too much to describe here, so spend time studying the finer details – it's better than money in the bank.

How to find and sell regular, reliable and repeat products – and avoid unsold stock cluttering up your home!

It's rarely *what* you sell that determines how successful you will be on eBay. Real success comes from *knowing what people actually want* to buy and finding items to satisfy their needs. And there's a lot of money to be won or lost in the process.

Learn from my experience. For my first main product, I chose cufflinks I liked – emphasis on *'I liked'*; I bought ten pairs of each, total 100 pairs at £5 a go. £500! With a resell price of £14.99, gross profit £9.99 each, I expected to triple or even quadruple my investment real fast. In practice I sold the odd pair, now and then, and soon found my selling fees way exceeded my takings. They eventually sold out at £4.99 a pair, less than I paid wholesale!

Today it's so different. Today I research products very carefully before even contemplating buying stock. Actually, I hardly ever buy stock before taking an order and I rarely create my own eBay pictures or sales materials.

I work out almost exactly what will sell before I even find the physical product and I've arranged with many product owners to let me sell their goods exclusively.

Study these few easy product selection tips, using cufflinks as our example:

- **Check what is currently in vogue by studying other people's listings for fastest selling items with multiple bidders and highest realisations.** It will take time but the end result can be fast, easy and certain high profits for everything you sell. For this example, I'd key 'cufflinks' into the search box top right of any eBay screen and study the results.

- **No one research method is best.** Success comes from researching and continually researching products, even those you've been selling for years, using all suitable tools at your disposal.

- **With a product in mind I turn to www.google.com**, my preferred search method, and key in such as 'cufflinks masonic wholesale'; 'masonic' being my chosen niche area. In practice I use various keywords, such as: 'cufflinks masonic pewter manufacturer', and so on, in hope of locating the majority of suitable suppliers for items I'd like to sell. I save search results rather than check sites upfront or list sites on paper. Copy me by creating a folder on your desktop to house your search results. When you've found a site you want to study later, go to 'File' and choosing 'Save as', opting as I do for 'Web Site' which lets you save pictures and all site details in one go. Make sure the results go in your folder or they'll be spewed all over your desktop.

- **Now begin visiting sites stored in your folder**, by clicking on the index files. You might find graphics are missing, depending on your software, but no matter for now. Check who the seller is and where they are based, prices, minimum order values if any, look for products most like those chosen from your earlier research. Make a shortlist of ten or so companies, ranked by your own first preference, second, and so on.

- **Particularly check sites with quality graphics** and try downloading graphics to your desktop in expectation of being allowed to do this by the seller. This isn't illegal unless you use the graphics for personal gain without permission. If the graphics aren't already stored in your folder, return to the site proper, point your cursor on a graphic, right click the mouse, choose 'save target as' and hopefully you'll see 'GIF' as an option. Locate your folder as the storing location and choose 'save' to store the graphic. Return to your desktop, open the folder, click on the icon. If it appears nice and clear then it's probably suitable for your eBay listing. Give it a suitable name to remember it by and move back to checking those suppliers' sites.

- **If the graphic is small it may be unsuitable for eBay listings**. Nothing looks worse than a skimpy graphic sitting amongst its bigger, bolder counterparts on eBay's listing pages. Go back to the product owner's site and click twice on your chosen graphic which very often grows bigger and more suitable for you. Otherwise ask owners for gif files for their products; most will accommodate.

- **For items you'd like to test-market, contact the supplier, tell them who you are and that you are planning to sell their products on eBay**. Request permission to use their graphics and maybe their sales spiel to sell their products. Most will more than happily agree. I've only ever had one refusal. I always confirm their approval by email and keep a copy for myself in case they 'change' their minds later.

- **List the item on eBay at the lowest possible price to cover product, selling fees and your own acceptable profit.** See how far bidding goes and if multiple bidders emerge. Calculate possible number of sales and eventual profits before the auction ends, and order the minimum possible quantity to fulfil orders. The first time I did this for pewter cufflinks, depicting carp figures for fishing enthusiasts, the results were profitable in the extreme. The cufflinks cost £5 a pair, two people were bidding and stopped at £60 and £62. Both eventually bought cufflinks that cost me £10 and brought £122 profits less selling fees. That doesn't happen every day, not with the same product, but it definitely does happen every day across a good range of, say, fifty or so products.

Finding a profitable niche

Many thousands of different items are listed on eBay each day in dozens of different categories.

As you'll discover, general categories – Collectibles, Music, Tickets and Travel – are sub-categorised, sometimes several times, ultimately to include a few select items in tight niche markets.

Selling to niche markets means lower overheads, higher profits, less work, less competition, unlimited potential.

These are the current main categories on eBay.co.uk's Home Page. Note that new categories are being added all the time, with wonderful benefits for niche marketers and others in general.

Current main categories

Antiques and Art
Automotive
Baby
Books, Comics, Magazines
Business, Office and Industrial
Clothes, Shoes, Accessories
Coins
Collectables / Collectibles
Computing
Consumer Electronics
Crafts
Dolls and Bears
DVDs, Film and TV
Health and Beauty
Home and Garden
Jewellery and Watches
Mobile and Home Phones
Music
Musical Instruments
PC and Video Gaming
Photography
Pottery, Porcelain, Glass
Sporting Goods
Sports Memorabilia
Stamps
Tickets and Travel
Toys and Games
Wholesale and Job Lots
Everything Else

Sub-categories

Click on one of those main categories to take you through to sub-categories which are niches in their own right but not quite so tight as those soon to come.

Here we'll consider a few main categories and their first generation sub-categories – Antiques and Art, Coins, Collectibles/Collectables.

Antiques and Art
Antiquities (currently a mammoth 2819 listings)
Architectural/Garden (currently 2257 listings)
Asian/Oriental
Carpets/Rugs
Clocks
Decorative Arts
Ethnographic
ETC.

Coins
Banknotes
Bullion/Bars
Coins
Historical Medals/Medallions
Share Certificates/Bonds
Tokens
ETC.

Collectibles
Advertising
Animals
Animation
Autographs
Badges/Patches
Bottles/Pots
Breweriana
Cigarette/Phone/Tea Cards
Decorative Ornaments/Plates
Disneyana
Ethnographic
Holiday/Seasonal
Household
Jukeboxes
Keyrings
Kitchenalia
Knives/Swords
Memorabilia
Metalware
Militaria
Moneyboxes/Piggy Banks
Paper and Ephemera
Photographic Images
Postcards
Radio/Television/Telephony
Religion/Spirituality
Rocks/Fossils
Royalty
Scientific
Science Fiction/Fantasy
Sewing/Fabric/Textiles
Tobacciana/Smoking
Tools and Hardware
Trading Cards
Trains/Railway Models
Transportation
Vanity/Perfume/Grooming
Vintage/Retro
Weird Stuff
Writing Equipment
Other Collectibles

Second generation sub-categories

Now look at sub-categories within one sub-category, in this case Collectibles > Advertising, those sub sections being:

Chemist
Distillery/Spirits
Drinks ..

.....and stop right there because within each, exampled here 'Drinks', there are further categories.

Third generation sub-categories

From Collectibles >Advertising >Drinks we find third generation categories:
Coca Cola
Cocoa
Coffee/Nescafe
Pepsi
Soft Drinks
Tea/Tetley

In this case, those final generations: Coca Cola, Cocoa, Coffee/Nescafe, Pepsi, Soft Drinks, Tea/Tetley are finely tuned niche markets for which thousands of collectors exist worldwide with few specialist dealers.

Consider specialising in one or more of countless niche markets and there's every chance you'll be the sole eBay specialist for those products and the main provider for thousands of collectors. Better still, by specialising in tight niche market products you'll find less competition from buyers at auctions, private sales, and similar, for your chosen product.

Buying at car boot sales and flea markets

These are wonderful places to buy (and sell), if you know what you're doing and you will know what you are doing as a regular subscriber to eBay Confidential. Flea markets and car boot sales are very similar events with the main exception that one is usually held indoors, the other outside.

Tips

- **Inspect sellers' stalls, especially inexperienced sellers at boot sales and flea markets.** You'll normally spot them from their haphazard approach to selling, unpriced goods, and hoards of pets running riot and kids fiddling with the stock! They usually offer the best bargains and will offer further discounts to ensure they sell out on the day and don't take unwanted stock back home.

- **Always haggle** with sellers, even for low value, high resale items. A caudle cup, priced at £5, haggled to £3, resold in Edinburgh recently for many thousands of pounds.

- **Arrive early** at fairs, swapmeets, markets, before other dealers get first pick of bargain goods and miracle finds. Say you're 'trade', even if you're not, and gain admission long before the doors open to the public.

- **Look for items now sold individually** which were originally issued in sets: some postcards, cigarette cards, some books. Find one and chances are the remainder are lurking alongside. For example, at a northern flea market I spotted a postcard showing what looked like part of Christ's face, followed soon by cards depicting other body parts – feet, hands, legs. Eventually I found twelve cards which I realised fitted together, in jigsaw fashion, to form Christ's body, with each card focusing on important events in the life of the Messiah. The cards, costing 20p each, were part of a 'composite set', which I kept, but is definitely worth hundreds of pounds.

- **Look for items that are poor sellers in one area** with high potential demand in another. Santa Claus postcards, for example, are hugely popular in America but just another postcard theme in Britain.

- **Learn about most desirable and high price collectable makes and makers** in your chosen field. Steiff for teddy bears, artists such as Kirchner and Mucha for glamour postcards and prints, Sutcliffe for early topographical photographs, Corgi for toys, etc.

- **Look for goods to buy in bulk which can be dismantled and sold individually.** Though still presenting competition from fellow dealers at auction or other selling venue, most collectors or dealers avoid buying in bulk when just a few items interest them. Postcards and stamps frequently come in bulk, in albums, as do boxes of books, toys, ephemera, and such. Likewise job lots, unwanted collections, and so on. For a recent example, the sale of items belonging to the late Dame Catherine Cookson featured hundreds of individual pieces, alongside trays and boxes packed with smaller less valuable goods, the likes of books, cutlery, small ornaments. For a few pounds per lot northern dealers acquired boxloads of items belonging to the north's most famous and best-loved daughter which were quickly cleaned, priced, and sold individually at flea markets, boot sales and from ads. in regional newspapers, not forgetting eBay where my own purchases sold like hot cakes in America.

Buying at liquidation and bankruptcy sales

Goods belonging to firms made bankrupt or liquidated are commonly auctioned to repay outstanding debts. That's bad for the failed business owner but great news for you and other eBayers. Our recent study of eBay PowerSellers showed a great many who specialise in one-type goods, such as tents, stationery, designer fashion, jewellery boxes and other packaging, catering equipment, being the very same items we found selling in massive job lots through offline auctions in our area next week.

Stock from liquidated or bankrupt, sometimes retirement sales, are usually passed to one or two local auctioneers you'll find advertising in local newspapers usually at the weekend.

Profit is rarely an issue on liquidated goods (from the Official Receiver, Bankruptcy Courts) and seized stocks (Customs & Excise, Inland Revenue) where sales are to raise money to repay creditors or to clear out long-standing stock in the auction house meaning reserves rarely apply.

Many sales are unadvertised so competition is low and goods often go for way below true market value.

Most importantly, by buying in bulk this way, at huge discounts, you'll have repeat items to offer regular customers and goods enough to keep your eBay shop permanently well stocked.

You could even start your own wholesale business

on eBay, by buying in bulk and selling in smaller quantities as many PowerSellers actually do. Even better, once attracted to your eBay wholesale listings you'll find many buyers contacting you outside of eBay for later acquisitions, meaning less time and energy spent listing new items. Make sure they don't contact you through eBay's communications channels, and don't you contact them that way, that's a big 'No-No' on eBay and could get you barred.

Other benefits

- **Many goods are new** – stock and business assets – especially from recently-failed start-up firms. They might also hold warranties with easy access to supplies and servicing.

- **Some auctions specialise**, say in one item (cars, property) or a single trade (catering, greetings cards and stationery, designer clothing). Your 'One Stop, Auction Stocking Shop' so to speak!!

Case Study: a colleague buys huge quantities of greetings cards and stationery, which are split and re-packaged and sold in wholesale quantities to market traders, car boot sellers, stationers and other retailers and, of course, on eBay! The same could easily apply to bulk sales of posters, jewellery, clothing, and so on.

Warnings

- **Beware ex-demonstration goods** (they could be damaged) – look for fingerprints and stains indicating heavy use.

- **Avoid other traders'** unsaleable stock (unlikely to sell for you, either) – check for sticky patches where price labels have been removed.

- **View goods from all angles** – and beat unscrupulous auctioneers' attempts to hide damaged goods by standing lots close to the wall, arranging items tightly together, placing items over heavy stains, painting over patched-up holes in cars and household goods.

- **Avoid items you can't inspect before bidding**, or risk buying computers that don't work, televisions and radios minus essential components, books with pages missing.

Introduction to Dropshipping – the easy way to sell hundreds of items on eBay without ever buying or holding any stock!

Imagine persuading big firms to invent, design and buy products, test the market, employ world class copywriters to describe their products, hire top-notch graphic designers and photographers – and give you the whole lot FREE OF CHARGE!

Well, that's exactly what you can do when you start using dropshipping as part of yoru ebay homee business. Here we reveal the inside strategies for getting this to work for you.

'Dropshipping' describes a process whereby a manufacturer or supplier delivers products directly to your customers without you ever needing to stock or pre-purchase goods.

Typically you list products on eBay, using your own or supplying companies' graphics and descriptions; you take payment, give the supplying company your buyers' names and addresses, and they send the product.

That's your part done; now you can go back to selling.

That's the theory, in practice it can be so different. Dropshipping is a wonderful way to make big money fast, and about the best way to lose money, too.

Sadly, it's a fact that many business owners care more about money than customer care and this can reflect badly for you, in the form of buyer complaints, poor quality products, long delays between customers paying and receiving their goods.

The onus is on you to take care of your business, and your customers, so be as careful picking dropshipping partners as you are planning all other aspects of your business.

More about dropshipping

- **Some so-called dropshipping offers border on scams**, asking a high fee to access a site, where you'll find more firms offering dropshipping information who in turn ask payment to access their sites, and so on, and so on. Where products are accessible with graphics and sales materials for your eBay listings, oftentimes the goods are rubbish, sometimes they're grossly overpriced. They might be seconds, end of line, customer returns, damaged... you get the picture!

- **That said, there are many excellent paid-for membership sites offering sound contact details for worldwide dropshipping companies**. Some membership sites continuously scrutinise their recommended suppliers, and score entries 1 to 5, acceptable to excellent, based on member feedback. The best we found, Worldwide Brands, is eBay acknowledged and operated by Chris Malta, Product Sourcing Editor of eBay Radio. The company has a team of researchers on constant lookout for new dropshipping and wholesale suppliers to add to their directory.

- **Find dropshipping companies yourself via their own advertisements in local newspapers** (not national; too competitive), at trade shows (*Trader* from newsagents lists the main ones), by word of mouth from sellers of non-competing products. Search for them online via search engines such as www.google.com (our preference); use appropriate kewords like 'manufacturers dolls (or other product) Durham (or other location)'.

- **Look for firms selling lots of different products, on a related or unrelated theme**. Within hours of deciding to sell dog featured jewellery, we searched www.google.com and found two firms willing to dropship their wide ranging products to our customers, with no minimum order, and a CD of graphics and sales materials arriving next day. Another firm, based a few miles from us, has more than twelve different products for over 100 breeds of dog, and no one currently selling their products on eBay! No graphics either, so we checked their products, bought one of each, and created our own unique listings.

- **Typically you pay the supplier an agreed amount per shipment upfront, although some will invoice you later.** For local firms you can pop down, offer their share, hand over delivery labels. When you have a good supplier, ask permission to pack goods yourself at their premises so you can insert special offer flyers, money-off vouchers. For distant suppliers keep close tabs on how well they serve your customers. See the next paragraph.

- **Negative feedback is much more likely using dropshipping and other partner companies than where you handle all customer transactions direct**. With the wrong partners you'll generate bad feeling, requests for refund, negative feedback, dismissal from eBay. Check partner companies by reading feedback from your customers. Look for problem delivery times, product quality concerns, poor customer service. Mounting negatives with similar complaints signify problems you must correct or seek new suppliers.

- **My experience of dropshipping has been exceptional.** I have companies posting products to my customers minutes after they get my faxed order and they always put my company details into the package, never their own. They don't poach my customers, they've never asked payment from me up front, they're better than I'd hoped for. Getting them was remarkably easy and all down to good communications. I telephone every potential dropshipper before promoting their products. I get to know the other person, determine how serious they are about their business, how approachable they are. Those I have chosen for my business talked more about customers and products than money, they were considerate and caring, keen to please. That first impression has always served me well. Do the same, you won't be disappointed.

- **If problems ensue, don't blame the dropshipper without checking first**. It could be you haven't explained your requirements properly, they may have serious business or personal problems, it could be coincidence or a batch of particularly difficult customers to blame for those negatives. Be careful, check thoroughly, and have an emergency plan for major problems. Have plenty of eggs in your basket: use several dropshippers, not just one, and have quality replacements waiting in line.

- **Sales materials and graphics are normally provided by larger suppliers or can be downloaded from their web sites**. Some have printed catalogues from which you can scan product pictures, others have CDs containing digital pictures. Using their pictures and descriptions makes life a lot easier for you; you won't spend time and money buying products, taking pictures, creating descriptions. But typically, the bigger the company, the more aggressive their marketing, and the more likely their products are known to other eBay sellers. The moral is don't rely solely on these bigger companies. Very often firms without sales materials and graphics are small companies, probably unknown to most other resellers, with fabulous products, and closer control over quality and communications. Of three companies providing my entire dog jewellery stock, two are one man set ups, the other a father and son business.

- **Good organisational and communications skills are needed, especially where you sell hundreds of different products from numerous dropshipping and supplying companies.** I've seen PowerSellers listing hundreds of thousands of products at one time, all totally different, and obviously from lots of individual suppliers. Imagine taking just one thousand orders a month (many eBayers take tens of thousands), and you must ensure each order reaches the correct fulfilment company, with accurate customer details, and proper payment. Complicated and very time-consuming. Far better sell a smaller range of high profit items from a few select suppliers.

- **Check competition on eBay for your dropshipping company and their products before planning to sell.** I found a wonderful dropship firm for CDs, there were hundreds of different titles, their graphics were bright and colourful, a more professional organisation was difficult to find. I joined their program, downloaded their graphics and sales materials, created and uploaded my listings, and waited, and waited, and nothing happened. Soon afterwards I checked for others selling similar products on eBay and found dozens of them. I should have checked first as in the next tip.

- **Search competition for your product by keying the name**, title or maker's name into the search box top right on eBay's home page. No entries for similar products might be good news for you, *might* because others *might* still be selling these products, just not right now. Bad news too because others might have tried selling similar products with little success. Lots of entries signals lots of competition, but view listings first to check similarity to your product. Where you find just a few people selling similar products, see how much they charge, check completed listings for how many sold and how many second chance offers were possible. More than five firms selling similar products worldwide, I'd say is one or two firms too many, except where they sell through auction and you choose shop only listings. If overseas firms sell similar products, but not internationally, consider selling in other countries.

Not quite dropshipping but every bit as good

• Artists and craftworkers are keen on making, not so keen on marketing, and are my favourite source of quality products. I make a point of visiting local craft fairs at least once a month where I find exhibitors selling stunning creations at a tiny fraction of eBay prices for similar items, if any exist. Many items are unique or limited edition and never get seen beyond a few miles of their makers' homes. My eldest daughter obtains designer jewellery this way, my youngest opts for hand-made dolls and teddies, and I take watercolour paintings on hand-made paper from a young Chinese artist whose work I sell exclusively on eBay. She dropships for me direct to my customers. Visit these fairs once and you'll return time and again. You don't have to buy items, most craftworkers and artists will work on commission, rather like a dropshipper who takes payment and delivers the product when you make a sale. Most will dropship to your customers. Find craftwork fairs advertised in local weekend papers, usually under 'Items for sale', 'Fairs and auctions', 'Days out', or similar. Find shops and static craft markets in *Yellow Pages* under 'Arts and Crafts', 'Artists', 'Art Organisations', 'Craft Shops and Galleries'. **Big Tip:** Among the most successful hand-made products on eBay are dolls' houses and dolls' house furniture, original animal paintings, wooden jewellery boxes.

Dropshipping tips from eBay's most successful powersellers

Dropshipping is a subject often mentioned in emails from our subscribers and it's clearly the preferred product sourcing method of most of you.

We've covered the subject several times already in past issues, if you missed them you can download our reports at www.1st-in-auctions.com/Dropshipping.html.

Each month we'll add more dropshipping tips for you, starting this month with advice from world-class eBayers and dropshipping specialists Janiece Smith and Dr. Brad. Beiermann.

JANIECE SMITH

In ***Don't Put All Your Eggs in One Basket*** Janiece Smith says:

> 'At least 99.99% of drop shippers sell their products for much more than you can buy them yourself right off eBay.
>
> But with a little work and a little knowledge, you can get the same products they sell for even cheaper than they do!'

This is how it's done:

1) Find a product category on a drop shipper's site that interests you and that you have some knowledge of.

2) Get an exact description of the product and the cost.

3) Conduct an eBay search for the exact product. If there are no current auctions for that product, try checking completed sales (Editor: Do this by going top right of the eBay screen, click on 'Advanced Search', next key product description in search box, tick 'completed auctions', then 'search').

4) Compare the sale price with the price for which you can purchase the item.

5) Make sure you compare the EXACT same product. Using a product that is close could include many variables that would make a difference in its sale price.

6) Check the shipping and handling prices for these products on eBay to make sure the seller is not low-balling the product's sale price and making his money on the handling fees.

7) If the product has a successful record of selling and is the exact same product that you're researching, then look a little closer as to whether you should list it or not.

8) If you decide to list it, make sure that (after you deduct all of your fees, including PayPal, eBay,

auction program, etc.) you are earning enough per hour to make it worth your while.

9) Choose an amount you will work for and don't get caught trying to sell items only to make $0.83 per hour. It will only waste your time. Spend your time finding high-profit, low-risk items.

10) If all the numbers work, sell the item! Then start trying to find new items and add more products.'

You'll find lots more tips from Janiece at www.1st-in-auctions.com/Janiece.html

DR. BRAD BEIERMANN

Dr. Beiermann specialises in assisting businesses find wholesale drop shipping companies and offers the following advice.

'These are the most common methods by which to find genuine drop shipping companies:

'**Internet Searches.** Doing an Internet search for a drop shipper has become one of the most widely used methods of finding a drop shipper. Many folks leverage the search engines to locate a desired product. After finding a specific product, they work their way backwards towards a search for a manufacturer listing the product. The manufacturer can sometimes be found by discovering several retailers selling the same product listing the name of a manufacturer. Once the manufacturer is discovered, a phone call can be made to find out about their distribution policies. (Editor: Notice here the author talks of locating the manufacturer, not a middleman drop shipping company and this is the very best way to find products at the lowest possible cost).

Trade Show Searches. (Editor: A great way to find products). Trade shows happen across the country in many major cities. There are many large shows that feature manufacturers and focus on a particular market segment (i.e. sporting goods, automotive, hardware... etc.). A trade show has the advantage of getting you face-to-face with manufacturers.'

For more information and advice from Dr. Beiermann, visit: www.hienote.com

Trade Shows – the best place to

find unique and unusual products to sell on eBay

Trade shows are a great place to find suppliers, generally manufacturers and wholesalers, but many are also happy to dropship their items directly to your customers. The reason they don't do this already is that they haven't been asked or they don't know how dropshipping works. It's your job to educate them.

The big secret to arranging exclusive dropshipping deals is to approach manufacturers and wholesalers face-to-face at trade shows.

Major trade shows have hundreds of exhibitors, it's like an Aladdin's Cave, there's so much to choose from, so many people to meet.

And, best of all, the vast majority of manufacturers are great at creating products but very poor at promoting their goods. They really need people like you, and me.

The secret to success is to act professionally, don't come across as someone desperately seeking something to sell, ***anything*** to sell as long as it gets them a little further out of debt!

Look closely at their goods before you approach stand holders. Scrutinise, look at things from all angles, try to look like an expert, a very picky expert. It's good to have someone with you, someone to talk quietly with about these people and their products.

Of course it's all a big show really, these products may be exactly what you want, but what the stall holders want is that you pay up front for their products or place a big order right away. Not good!

At my first trade show I made the mistake of buying one of each item on some stalls, hundreds of cufflinks from one stall, four hundred dog pendants from another. I spent about £4,000 that day, because I was new to eBay and thought this is what 'proper' eBayers do. Wrong, wrong, wrong, I still have more than £3,000 worth of stock tying up space in my garage more than two years later. I can't even sell at the price I paid.

It's much different now. With experience, and having made some great trade contacts, I now realise manufacturers need people like you and me much more than we need them.

They're great at making things, remember, and lousy at marketing.

Just take my word for it, you're much more important than you might think right now.

Visit a few trade shows, learn the ropes, and we'll give more tips for approaching suppliers in our weekly ezines and monthly newsletters.

Useful addresses and sources of further information

You'll find lots of information about trade shows at: www.businesslink.gov.uk – type 'trade show' into their search box top right of the screen.

For a comprehensive events and dates diary for trade shows and other trade events, visit www.exhibitions.co.uk

Introduction to the import business

Imagine millions of great products to choose from, cheaper than anything you've seen before, good quality, you've already tested them on eBay, proved they're great sellers, the mark up is huge and, best of all, there's no one else selling anything remotely similar to all the hundreds of items you're selling on eBay, week in week out!

Sounds perfect doesn't it? And in fact it is perfect, and easily achievable too, especially if you learn the easy process of buying goods overseas for selling in your own country, and possibly developing a sole agency agreement with your provider which means no one else can sell those items but you.

Import is a business almost anyone can operate profitably with few skills and little capital required.

Import simply means introducing a product available in one country to another country, not necessarily your own. So you could, for example, import jewellery from Hong Kong to New Zealand without ever leaving the UK or taking possession of the product.

The process is simple, very simple, and on eBay it's as easy as buying products from Australia, on eBay.au or eBay.com, having them sent to your home in the UK, where you list and sell them on eBay.co.uk.

You could import from any eBay country site and sell on another eBay country site, by taking possession of the items in the UK or operating with drop-shipping companies outside the UK willing to send your products to other countries also outside the UK.

That is import at its simplest, and it's a wonderful way to grow an eBay business.

All but the newest eBayers might already have purchased goods from overseas on eBay. The bidding process is the same as for buying from UK sellers, you might bid in foreign currency but you'll probably pay in pounds using intermediary company PayPal. The goods arrive, probably in the same post as items from UK sellers, they'll probably just take a little while longer on route.

The only possible complications and financial costs are import taxes, VAT, and the fact that some products are unsuitable outside their country of origin, some are illegal.

We'll cover the basics of import here, there's much more to learn, none of it difficult, and experience will be your best guide.

The first, most important step is to choose a product you'd like to work with. Take time over this essential feature of the business.

Ideas

Go to www.ebay.com, key 'wholesale' into any search box. Today you'll get 41,198 listings having the word 'wholesale' in their title. This is how I would use that information:

• **Click on 'Wholesale Lots'**. There are 8,222 entries. Click on any, I chose the first, and was taken to a seller, in the UK, selling wholesale watches and jewellery. I checked feedback, not bad at all, looked at his other items, and found lots of items in big bundles that should easily sell individually or batched with other of my products. Most important of all, I found a specialist wholesale seller in the UK, someone I'll record for future perusal.

• **Under 'Sporting Goods Wholesale'** I found football shirts, golf balls, martial arts clothing, fishing lures. All brand names, no bids, all just minutes to go, all priced ludicrously low. Come Christmas those items will sell like hot cakes and will go into gift baskets I have planned for the big spend season.

More product tips

The product must be capable of selling at a decent profit, or there's no sense in importing it. Unless your chosen product is really unique you can study other eBayer's listings of similar products. Enter your product description, top right of eBay's pages, you'll be taken to current listings. Study bidding prices, number of bidders, listing strategies. Do an advanced search, again top right of eBay's pages, tick 'Completed Listings', enter your product description, and you'll see all similar items, sold and unsold over the past few weeks.

The right product for you to import is one which is either newer, or better, than an existing product or something you can sell cheaper or with added benefits, such as better customer service, a useful free gift, good choice of colours, two for the price of one.

Winning example

My daughter had trouble selling her framed dog prints after other eBayers copied her idea and almost depleted her market. Undaunted, she located an eBayer in the US selling dog pins and brooches at about £1 each. She imported them and gave a pin free of charge with every dog print sold. She made a big thing of the free gift, even placing a cameo picture of the pin bottom left of the print, in its stylish little box, also obtained inexpensively on eBay. Bottom line: sales are up again and rising, competitors sales are flagging.

Choosing products

Choosing a product you are already familiar with, maybe something you are a customer for, gives you the edge over operating with products about which you know little or nothing.

Other important considerations include whether the product is seasonal, like toys, or if you might expect to trade in it all year round. And you'll need to know that your product is reliable and safe and that spare parts and repair services are available in your buyers' country. Local Customs and Excise officers will answer questions and you could also visit your local office or telephone for lots of useful information about international trade. Find details in local telephone directories or visit the HM Revenue and Customs site at: http://www.uktradeinfo.com.

Finally, it is usually the cost of an overseas product and its home-produced rival that decides whether or not yours is a suitable import. Some countries have lower production and labour costs than Britain, representing enormous savings for British importers. You must be careful, however, because cheap doesn't always mean good. In fact, cheap can sometimes mean the authorities will seize your product and condemn it as unsuitable for the domestic market. Check quality always, especially where prices are low.

Generally regarded as 'safe' for newcomers:

Few of the items listed here cause problems for seller or buyer, but you must still check carefully before importing fabrics that might be flammable or big name jewellery that turns out to be fake. Where in doubt obtain a few samples to check before buying in bulk.

Crafts, gifts, etc.
Novelties (subject to quality).
Travel goods.
Photographic equipment.
Tools.
Jewellery.
Clothing and fabrics.
Household goods.

Try to avoid:

Electrical goods – they may fall below required safety standards or be unsuitable for use in some countries.

Toys – may not be up to standard for the UK's rigid toy quality and safety laws.

Foodstuffs – need a special licence, difficult to sell, might perish fast in transit.

Animals and livestock – need special licence, not usually suitable for resale on eBay.

Plants and agricultural products – need special licence and some plants are prohibited from entering certain countries due to laws affecting drugs and plant borne diseases.

Heavy or bulky goods – cumbersome and costly to transport.

Fragile and perishable items – easily broken or ruined in transit.

Poor quality goods – for obvious reasons.

Very low cost items where a high volume must be sold to achieve a profit – obvious.

Discontinued items – no after sales service, limited spares, low repeat business.

Finding a supplier

Let us assume you know what you want to sell. Now you have to decide whether to concentrate on this one product or import a range of related or spin-off products. Most importantly, in the beginning, you should resist the urge to offer a range of unrelated products. You'll get confused and you'll probably spread your efforts too thin to give your business any real chance of success.

Next you will have to find a supplier – manufacturer, ebay seller, overseas exporter, or other – for the product.

The following are the most common ways to source overseas suppliers:

• **Approach embassies and foreign trade representatives**, including London and other city based foreign chambers of commerce. Look in London telephone directories for embassy details. When you have the appropriate contact, it's simply a matter of writing or telephoning for the information you need, namely a list of suppliers in their country for the kind of product you are interested in.

• **Look in appropriate trade journals and import/export journals where write ups and advertisements feature for suppliers offering goods direct or asking for agents to represent them overseas.** You'll find everything you need at local business libraries. These are not the same as local public libraries or reference libraries but they can give you details of your local business library.

Virtually all major towns and cities have one.

• **Attend trade fairs.** Here, you will probably meet the manufacturer face-to-face as well as being able to see, touch and discuss the product. Numerous fairs are held regularly throughout the world, sometimes dealing in one type of product, frequently covering all kinds of goods. A great many foreign manufacturers also exhibit at UK trade fairs.

• **Take a break**, visit the country involved, speak to suppliers, spend time sourcing additional products to sell. If you bring samples home you must inform Customs officials when you re-enter the UK. They will calculate import duties and whatever other charges are appropriate.

• **On eBay.** With so very much available on the world's largest market place, you may never have to look elsewhere.

• **Other.** Spend time searching web sites including eBayers also marketing outside of eBay, look in national and international wholesale directories, and other areas we'll mention in future newsletters.

If you haven't done so already, need to make contact with the supplier. This can be done by letter, telephone, fax, email.

Ask for samples, even if that means paying for them. Use PayPal if you can as this offers some protection against fraud and non-delivery.

Checking the product

Once you have chosen your product there are still a number of things to take into account before attempting to sell.

• **Price.** Is it competitive in relation to quality and price of similar goods in your target market? Remember to include all costs: price from manufacturer, transport costs, customs and excise duties.

• **Is the product legal?** Does it conform to national standards?

• **What competition is there** for the product in your target market?

• **Is potential demand large enough** to make it worth your while importing the item?

• **Is the product technically suitable, where appro-**

priate? For example, voltage systems vary by country, broadcast systems (certain radios and video systems can not be used in some other countries).

Import duties, taxes, etc.

This was the feature of the import process that bothered me most which in fact is not complicated and involves you doing little or nothing except sometimes paying money when money is due.

Import duties sometimes apply based on sending country, value of product, type of product, and the subject is far too wide to discuss here, so you'll find links to sites offering specialist information at the end of this article.

Some items will be subject to import taxes, if they exceed a specific value and unless they are marked as 'gift' or as having no commercial value. For example, recently I ordered 100 Masonic brooches from an American seller. He chose to send the items in two separate packages, mainly to avoid the entire bundle getting lost in the post. When the packages arrived, the postman requested import tax of ten pounds on one of the packages, the other travelled tax free. The reason was a tiny difference in the value of the two packages and, when opened by Customs as many items are, officers decided the item had commercial value, which it did, and levied a tax. The threshold for import duties to apply is currently £18 from non-EU countries.

Note that all packages sent or received from overseas should carry a Customs Declaration Form – CN 22 – indicating their value. Customs will let some items go through unchecked even with a Customs sticker.

Importantly, import duties can be deducted from profits for tax purposes.

The Post Office will not release imported parcels until duty and VAT have been paid in full, even if duty relief has been granted or if VAT exemption applies.

I will admit I never check what import duties or VAT are payable on anything I buy from overseas. If I've done my homework properly I'm going to make decent profits anyway and almost certainly import duties from non-EU countries will be far lower than their VAT charging country counterparts. As a VAT registered trader I can claim back VAT spent on

goods for my business but, quite frankly, I'd import suitable products even where I couldn't reclaim.

Finally

Import takes on various guises, the easiest and least risky being that already described where you decide on a product, find a supplier, then arrange the transaction direct.

About sole agents

A sole agent is the only person allowed to sell a specific item in a particular location. Belonging more to the world of traditional import, where agents mediate between buyer and seller and may never see the items they sell, the Internet, specifically eBay, has led many manufacturers to accept eBay sellers as sole agents, creating massive market potential for people like you and me.

But, you must not rush to sign a sole agency agreement. It's best to test the product first and make sure it sells before entering into an agreement which might prohibit you from selling similar or competing products in your target area.

Sources of further information

http://www.out-law.com

Strangely named, www.out-law.com has lots of useful information about Value Added Tax, Import Duties and other financial matters surrounding importing products to and from various countries.

HM Customs and Excise (HMCE) – www.hmrc.gov.uk.

Their site says: 'For goods moving within the EU, import duties and taxes do not usually apply. However, for goods imported from non-EU countries, Customs charges do apply, these may include import duty, excise duty and import VAT. Goods with a value exceeding £18 (for commercial items including internet/mail order purchases), or £36 in the case of gifts between private individuals, are generally subject to Customs charges. Normally charges are calculated upon the declared value (plus postage for commercial items)'.

HMRC's National Advice Centre – 0845 010 9000

'Ring for detailed information on import customs

procedures and charges. In this section there are some guidelines for customers importing parcels into the UK. Importing into the UK is usually straightforward, but there may be times when it becomes more complicated given the contents of the packages, or the reasons for import.'

www.royalmail.co.uk
www.postoffice.co.uk

Both sites provide lots of useful information regarding cost of sending and receiving international mail.

Business Libraries

Ask details of your local business libraries at local public and reference libraries or telephone your local county town hall.

Foreign and Commonwealth Office –
http://www.fco.gov.uk

Provides a list of addresses and contact details for all UK-based Embassies and Consulates.

UK Trade and Investment Office –
http://www.uktradeinvest.go.uk

Provides a long list of information and contact details for overseas companies for the purpose of import and other trade connections.

Trade Fairs and Exhibitions UK –
http://www.exhibitons.co.uk

Diary and contact details for trade fairs and exhibitions in the UK

Selling other people's goods on commission – also known as 'The Consignment Business' 'Trading Assistant Programme' and 'Drop Off Shops'.

We've covered various means of selling on eBay without having stock of your own to sell. The best options are dropshipping, using small scale wholesalers, and selling on commission.

The latter, where others pay you to list their goods and you also take a share of the proceeds is perhaps the easiest and most profitable option. So called 'drop off shops' are big in the USA and almost non-existent in the UK. It's a great business to move into quickly and even corner a huge chunk of the British market.

To quickly recap on earlier issues, the business works like this:

• **You promote your service to private individuals and business owners who for some reason can't or don't want to sell items personally on eBay**. Having your own web site is essential and it must fit certain requirements.

• **Potential vendors visit your site, read your conditions**, check your product requirements, see how much you charge to sell their goods.

• **They contact you, describe what they have to sell**, confirm agreement to your conditions, leave the product or samples with you for photographing, describing, listing and eventually delivering to winning bidders.

• **You list, communicate with enquirers and bidders**, take payment, process goods, send a portion back to vendors.

So easy, it's almost childlike, but only if you carefully pre-plan your business, and you can do that based on already successful consignment sellers working mainly in America and Canada.

Website Essentials

This is where most vendors' first impressions about you are formed. Your site has to look good, instill confidence, it should lay out exactly what you expect of vendors and what they can expect of you.

At http://auctionbytes.com/cab/pages/consign I found links to hundreds of American and Canadian consignment sellers, including some promoting a handful of things each week and others with bases all over America.

This is what I learned from my research:

• **A plain, simple, easy-to-navigate page is essential**. Potential vendors are confused already about the auction and consignment business, otherwise they'd be running their own eBay ventures. There were some really great sites on the list alongside some that were nothing short of unsightly. Sorry, www.ridyourstuff.com, but I really couldn't make head or tale of your site, I'm sure many vendors will feel the same.

• **www.treasuresrecycled.com** – one of the prettiest and user-friendliest of sites I found. Treasures Recycled have been in the business of estate and antiques for more than 25 years and selling on eBay since 1998 with a total of over 21,000 positive feedbacks and rising daily. Every so often I find a company I'd love to emulate, this is one of them. Take a look, you'll soon understand why.

• **www.bidbrothers.com** is another simple site which provides a gallery of items already sold on consignment, with prices achieved, even buyer feedback for interested vendors to check and dispel all worries about doing business this way.

• **The best sites included logos showing their status as eBay Trading Assistants**. Some even used eBay's distinctive colours: bright blue, green, yellow and red on their home page, being careful not to breach trademark and copyright laws. See how it's done at www.yourauctionpros.com and www.auctioncafe.net

• **Also on www.auctioncafé.net**, when visitors click 'Enter' there's a table showing exactly how much the vendor receives from sales of their product. http://www.quikdrop.com/fees.php is another site that shows exactly what both parties receive to the transaction and helps potential vendors decide between selling on their own or hiring a professional seller.

• **Proving size can be a problem**, at www.Ztradingpost.com, they have outlets all over the USA, and on the day I looked hardly any of their links were working. There's a tip: check your site regularly, make sure visitors don't discover mistakes before you do.

• **One of best I saw, with eBay colours**, logos, simplicity, even a 'check the status of your auctions' feature is www.cluttertocash.net. When I grow up on eBay I want to be just like them. Go on take a look, you'll be very pleased you did!

Building a business with intention to sell

• **First on the list of US and Canadian companies**, www.1stopauctions.com is up for sale, it seems because the business has grown too big to handle alongside an existing real estate business. I'm not suggesting you buy it, the intention is to show how such a business, developed from little or no capital, can generate a hich ticket resellable product, namely the business itself.

You can build up and sell an eBay business just like any other venture, on and off the Internet. So not only can you be making good money today, but you're also building something for the future, for your children, as a source of retirement income, just for a lump sum to enjoy your golden years.

Promoting your consignment business

A simple postcard in a shop or post office window, or a small classified advertisement in your local paper should bring all the business you need in the early days.

These are samples you can adapt for your business.

Postcard for Shop Window.

Let an experienced eBay trading assistant sell your unwanted household goods

We specialise in toys, designer clothing, paper collectibles, blah, blah, blah

Small Fee and Commission Basis

Telephone: xxxxx xxxx xxxx
Email: xxxxxxxxxxxxxxxxxxxxxxxxxxxxxxxxxxxxxxxx

Sample Classified Advertisement

Let Us Sell Your Goods on eBay. Private and business owners contact experienced eBay Trading Assistant. (Put email address, phone number, box number, web site url at the end of advertisement).

Tips

- **Do not give your address on postcards or in advertisements**. You'll attract time-wasters, curiosity seekers and even burglars who suspect your place is packed with valuable antiques and collectibles. A newspaper box number is also a good idea which can be arranged with newspaper advertising staff. Or you might consider opening a post office box; ask for information at your local post office.

- **Place newspaper advertisements on Friday and Saturday**. This leaves the weekend for you to respond quickly to enquirers while their interest is hot. It also means you can go view goods which is usually easier at the weekend than weekdays.

- **Always use 'Us' and 'Our Company' in all sales materials**. It makes you look bigger than you are; more reliable, less likely to be dodgy. A recent report about freelance consultants suggested those who worked on their own, under their personal name, received fewer assignments than others seemingly working as part of a larger company. It seems customers like the security of someone else to deal with their work and problems if you are on holiday or fall sick. Strangely, that confidence also applied to one-man or woman businesses using a company name instead of their own, suggesting the business is bigger than it really is. So instead of calling your consignment business 'Iman eBay-Seller', go with something like 'IMA Group' or 'Littletown Trading Post', or similar.

Useful information

eBay Trading Assistants Program Tools and tips for consignees.
http://www.ebay.com/tatoolkit

Resale World Consignment Software
Offers software for consignment stores and eBay Trading Assistants.
http://www.resaleworld.com/

Big time trading assistants

But these aren't small time eBayers, these people actually earn tens of thousands of pounds from just one sale. They're selling aeroplanes, ships, properties, complete business setups, valuable antiques and collectors' items.

Don't rush off, don't think you have to be an expert to earn huge commissions selling unusual items like this.

The simple fact is, most people selling rare and one-off items know little or nothing about the items themselves; their skills lie in describing, listing and selling high ticket items and earning excellent commissions each time.

Facts

It's easier to sell to someone with money to spend than to someone who has little or nothing.

To which I would add:

It's just as easy to sell one high ticket item as lots of tiny low cost items.

In fact, selling that one high ticket item could be a whole lot easier than continuously listing new items for sale each week which involves:

• **Lots of work and attention to detail**, long hours possible, numerous questions to answer from potentially hundreds of people.

• **Listing fees**, though cost-effective, can still represent a large chunk of your takings for the week.

• **More problems likely to make life just that little bit more unpleasant**, such as non-payers, negative feedback, complaints about products not arriving, and so on.

• **More likelihood of relying on others**, namely manufacturers and dropshippers, to process orders direct to your customers, and consequently more potential delivery problems.

I'm not backing out on what I've said before about eBay being a numbers game, and the more items you list, the more items you'll sell, and the more money you'll make.

I firmly believe that and I actually enjoy listing

goods on eBay. But anyone with little time or who doesn't enjoy sitting at the computer for several hours each day should look at selling higher priced items on commission.

One of the most famous and successful people in this business is Don Peters of San Antonio, Texas.

Don has taken the commission selling business to a really high level, having sold aeroplanes, boats, time shares, even inflatable churches, personal bunkers and very high end antiques.

He's been commission selling since 1999 and says his target market is: 'Anyone willing to spend 6 figures and above to buy unusual items found on eBay'. Outside of eBay he markets unusual and unique items at www.airplanehomes.com and www.iwillsellyourstuff.com.

He's an ardent marketer and works hard to get traffic to his web sites and eBay listings, by sending press releases about his products, using Google AdWords and other pay per click promotions, and spending as long as it takes to create really detailed auction listings and lots of great pictures for his products.

It's a business anyone can start and succeed in, either independently or as a recognised eBay Trading Assistant. Trading Assistants receive a special logo to highlight their status and lots of useful information provided by eBay. Read more about eBay's Trading Assistant Scheme at: http://pages.ebay.co.uk/tradingassistants/hire-trading-assistant.html

Advice

• **Remember listing and final fees increase in line with starting and finishing prices for your product.** Listing and finishing fees for high value items can reach hundreds even thousands of pounds a time. Decide who is responsible for eBay fees before you start work on your listings. Most sellers make vendors pay all costs associated with the sale, before their own commission is deducted. Some share the cost, but rarely does the commission seller shoulder the entire burden. Have individual responsibilities clearly laid out in the commission agreement.

• **Unlike listing 500 items each week**, in confidence of half or more selling, you will be listing far fewer items with possibly long spells between sales. Help keep the cash flowing by continuously seeking new high-ticket items or spend part of your time listing less profitable products with high success potential.

- **On the plus side**, you never have to pay out for products that don't actually sell. The vendor takes all the risks. But you must agree terms in advance and ensure the vendor's expectations are realistic. If vendors set their prices too high, you risk more unsuccessful listings.

- **You don't need to be an expert on the product you are selling**, as long as the owner or someone close can provide information and advice to form the basis of your listing. If in doubt, choose vendors with specialist knowledge of products for you to sell.

eBayers selling mainly high ticket items, usually on a commission basis, include:

- **4auctionhelp** is currently promoting a car valued at $55,000 and invites people to contact them for help selling their items.

- **Rsus is selling a Ferrari priced at $142,300** and there are already bids exceeding $100,000.

- **A mausoleum resting place for 2 in Tampa Florida** is not attracting bids yet for Trading Assistant bidwayusa whose past record of selling other people's items is littered with high profit deals.

My thanks go to John M Evans, author of *Success Alert: Conversations With Successful Internet Entrepreneurs* for information about Don Peters. You can find more information about John's book at: www.1st-in-auctions.com/SA.html

Tips

Terry Gibbs advises:

- **'By selling other people's items you learn the value of items in the most practical way**. By handling them and selling them. No matter how many price guides you read, and antique shows you attend, you will never get the feel for items until you sell them.

- **When you sell on consignment, you provide a service that makes your clients additional money**. When most people sell something, they sell

to a dealer who needs to mark up the item to make a profit. This is not what happens on eBay.

- **You need to take possession of the items.** When you sell items on consignment you risk your eBay name and reputation. You take these risks when you sell your own items, but you are in complete control of your actions. In order to lower your risks you need to get complete control of the items you are going to be selling. This prevents sellers from changing their minds, and allows you to ship the items as soon as you receive payment.'

But how do you get people to part with their valuable items?

It's much easier than it sounds, and the process is no different to thousands of people parting with their goods for offline auction houses to describe and sell. Offline auction houses and some postal sellers take items, make a quick estimate of value, return this estimate to vendors who are asked to sign their approval to sell the items. Those items remain with the auction company.

It's more difficult for newcomers to take possession this way especially those lacking feedback or experience of auction selling.

You could build feedback and reputation quickly by purchasing lots of cheap items on eBay and getting sellers to leave feedback right away. You might sell items for family and friends and get them to recommend you to other people. In practice you'll probably find lots of people willing to part with low value items and build up to more expensive items later.

As you move into high value items you must have a contract which both parties sign. This protects you against vendors fraudulently misrepresenting their goods or pulling out of a sale.

A simple contract will suffice, stating that you will do your best to achieve a high price for the product and pass relevant monies back to the vendor at an agreed time after the sale. For his part the vendor acknowledges title or rights to offer you the product based on descriptions provided to the best of his knowledge.

There's a sample agreement letter for you to download at: www.1st-in-auctions.com/Agreement.html. This is similar to one I use which I created myself, and is offered for information and advice only, and not as a legally binding document. For high price products you should have a solicitor prepare a contract for you.

Terry Gibbs is a collector/dealer of old toys and trains, and teaches others how to buy and sell antiques and collectibles. You can read the remainder of this and other excellent articles by Terry at: www.1st-in-auctions.com/TerryGibbs.html

The best place to buy all the stock you ever need... without once leaving home

One of the very best places to buy stock is on eBay itself. This may sound strange, but many of eBay's most successful sellers, some turning over thousands of items each month, obtain most of their stock through eBay.

Let's see what's involved and how you can buy high profit items cheap without ever leaving home.

• **Some eBayers have several accounts**, some for buying activities, others strictly for selling. Many have just one account for all their buying and selling activities, for business and personal use. These are the easiest to study. When you find someone selling a lot of the type of products you'd like to sell, click on one of their listings and at the right side go to 'read feedback comments'. Click on feedback 'From Sellers' and you'll see exactly what your subject buys on eBay, how often, where from, at what price.

• **Note IDs of your subject's regular suppliers or add them to your favourite sellers**. Check feedback for your subject's main suppliers, look for other regular buyers, especially of multiple lots. Concentrate on resellers rather than personal buyers, check how successful these people are, what items sell best and attract highest prices.

• **Profit from other people's mistakes**, such as items listed in inappropriate categories, consequently attracting few bidders and low finishing prices. Finding these mistakes is more down to good luck and careful research than anything else but the results can be hugely profitable and available

entirely to you. I spend at least one hour every day searching eBay, looking for profitable items attracting few bids. Sometimes I bid on those items, more often not, but I always earn more from that one hour than all the time spent acquiring stock outside of eBay.

• **Look regularly for last minute listings with few or no bidders in your favourite product category. Bank holidays**, late at night, very early in the morning, when something important is happening like a Royal Wedding or major sporting event, bidder turnout is often low and some amazing bargains are possible.

Mail order returns!

Some local and regional auction houses deal specifically or generally in items returned by large mail order catalogue companies. Most returned goods are in good condition, with just the package opened, sometimes with slight faults, more often they're perfect specimens.

It isn't worthwhile for large mail order companies like Great Universal and Littlewoods to return goods to stock, so they sell for a tiny fraction of their real worth at auction.

Find auction houses selling mail order goods in your area by looking in local and regional newspapers, usually at the weekend. Make a note of frequent sellers and telephone regularly about forthcoming events.

More and more auction houses are posting their catalogues online so you can stay up-to-date on what's selling.

Further information

• **For overstocks including mail order returns go to**: www.stockshifters.co.uk

• **Most larger regional newspapers have a specialist auction section listing auctions houses and forthcoming sales**, including some specialising in mail order returns. Look in the contents pages for separate listings or for smaller local papers look under 'Auctions' among the classifieds. Alternatively, find local papers listed in *Yellow Pages* and ask about auction listings. In *Yellow*

Pages, under 'Auctions' phone sale rooms closest to you. Ask if they auction mail order returns and if not, who does. Most auctioneers happily recommend their non-competing counterparts.

Quarter of a million sales per month – too much for you to handle?

Not if you choose products carefully!

I don't know about you, but I'd love to be selling thousands of items a month, although 24,000 might be a few thousand too many for most small ventures to handle. But it can be done, as eBayer pugster888 will testify.

They've been selling charms on eBay since 2002, just three years, and any day now they're set to hit the 1 MILLION positive feedback mark. The company received almost half a million feedbacks in the past twelve months, just 404 of them negative.

Charms represent one of numerous items with high multiple and repeat purchase potential, I reckon the average sale for Pugster888 is 7 to 8 charms per buyer.

More than this, charms are one of the most popular products on eBay, get it right and few items go unsold and, even if unit profits are low, cumulative profits can be quite spectacular.

Another benefit of multiple purchase, fast turnover items like charms, is that once listed an item can remain in your listings and continue selling week after week, year after year. Not forgetting that, find someone manufacturing a wide range of charms (or other multiple purchase item) and you have just one place to go for stock. Set up a good trading relationship with that manufacturer and they might even produce products exclusively for you.

Why am I telling you this? Simply to introduce

you to a host of examples of products typically manufactured over a large range of designs, often inexpensive to buy with relatively good profit margins, typically lending themselves to fast turnover, repeat purchase, constant replenishment.

These products should fit the bill:

- Fishing lures.
- Brooches, pins, charms.
- Craftwork supplies.
- Jewellery Making Findings, Beads, etc.
- Greetings cards.

Selling affiliate products on eBay

A strange title, 'Selling Affiliate Products on eBay', because it's against eBay's rules to sell purely affiliate products via traditional means. By 'traditional' I mean adding affiliate links in your listings and getting people to pay someone else for the product, namely the supplier, through your affiliate link.

The buying and selling contract is between eBay members, not outsiders, a rule eBay enforces to the hilt. Quite rightly so!

There are ways to get round the problem, honestly and legally, and you can sell the same products and earn similar or higher commissions as regular affiliates for the supplying company.

Let me explain from experience.

This week I opened a pet shop. Not a high street pet shop, mine is an eBay pet shop, selling all manner of items, some small, others too big for most people to store, pack and post from home.

I reckoned if firms seek affiliates to promote their products from web site links, they should also be receptive to other reseller deals. I put my theory to the test, starting with companies I found via affiliate middleman affiliatewindow.com from where I source most of my affiliate products.

I found two companies, one selling smaller items, like homeopathic medicines, dog leads and collars, books, gifts for animal lovers. The other company manufactures large kennels and runs and other bulky items for dogs spending most of their time outdoors.

Both offered 20 per cent commission on sales made by affiliates through traditional web site links.

I emailed both and posed an alternative selling proposition.

'Can I market your products on eBay, use your graphics and sales materials, and pay you direct to send your products to my customers, after I have deducted my twenty per cent share of the takings?'

Both agreed.

How easy was that? I looked further into ways to sell affiliate products without breaking eBay rules. This is what I came up with.

Using reports to promote affiliate products and back end sales

You could write a short report, or have someone else write one for you or take it from the public domain, focusing on some important matter affecting potential buyers of high commission affiliate products. The report, designed mainly to attract enquiries and a mailing list for more expensive products, can be priced to just cover your eBay expenses and include affiliate links for readers who might ultimately buy those other products. Fifty pence to two or three pounds are common for these short reports which are offered on CD or as downloads.

These reports might appeal to subsequent big ticket buyers.

- *Help Your Child Pass Important Exams* – the booklet includes revision tips, the importance of a healthy eating and sleeping regime, memory jogging tips, and so on. The booklet might also promote exam revision weekends, educational software, books and revision courses.

- *Secrets of Ageless Ageing* – a short report on how strong sunshine, smoking, drinking and unhealthy eating cause premature ageing. The report also promotes skin care products, health farm visits, books, cosmetic surgery.

Using your 'About Me' page

You are not allowed to redirect visitors from your eBay listing to other sites with the intention of selling outside of eBay. But you can invite people to visit your About Me page and even provide information that leads to a non-eBay sale.

Here's an idea to help you get started.

Give an interesting title to your listing that encourages the reader to open your listing. For example:

KEEY YOUR CAT SAFE – Battery Powered Location Tracking Device. Buy It Now £3.99.

The title plays on every cat lover's concern for their pet's safety. Many people will visit to see just what this wonderful product is that costs so little. Inside your listing you direct people to your About Me page to read all about another great product you have just acquired, costing a great deal more than £3.99. Here you can give links to other web sites and you'll probably sell a few of those £3.99 products too.

Five tips to help you successfully find products at below wholesale prices

By Janiece V Smith

Most people think a wholesaler is 'the' place to get all of the good deals and the cheapest products. This is not always true. Many times, products are not even sold through a wholesaler.

Some manufacturers sell their overstock, closeout, and liquidation items through wholesalers. Some wholesalers (and manufacturers. Editor) sell their items through outlets; others sell them on their own. Some wholesalers (manufacturers, too) have exclusive divisions that deal only with a handful of people who prove themselves as reliable sources who can move inventory fast.

You should always try to first get your products from the top source (usually the manufacturer. Editor). Don't waste your time dealing with others who have marked up the product many times before it ever gets to you. Many companies have a set way to move their unsold inventory, so, sometimes, going to the top might not work as smoothly as you want.

Don't get discouraged if these companies already have clients they sell the bulk of their stock to. You can still get the product; it will just be a little further down the line.

Here are five ways to help you find the products you are looking for.

- **Ask manufacturers who you should speak with to purchase unsold inventory.** They will normally guide you in the right direction. Be aware that sometimes finding the right contact can take a little arm twisting.

- **Find out what manufacturers currently do with their unsold inventory.** Who do they sell it to if they don't sell it themselves? If they won't disclose this information or act like they don't want to deal with you, find a different approach.

- **Find out whether they sell to the general public** and what they require of you and your company to be able to buy their products.

- **Next, find out which products they sell to the public**. Most companies have some products they will not release as unsold inventory. They would rather try to resale it on their own.

- **Make sure you have all of your ducks in a row**. Most, if not all, of the manufacturers I deal with don't want to play games. They want to move their products and they want to move them fast. Just make sure you know what you want, be confident when you make that call, and have a goal that you want to accomplish. If you call and sound like you don't know what you are doing, they will quickly shut you out.

To read more of Janiece's ideas, go to: www.1st-in-auctions.com/Janiece.html

Our special niche marketing report, packed with ideas for researching best selling products, is still available for our subscribers only at: www.1st-in-auctions.com/Niche.html

Our tips to tthe top

Some wholesalers and manufacturers want to sell purely to established businesses and not to members of the public. But, of course, everyone has to start somewhere, so how do you create this impression of 'respectability' if this is your first business venture? These tips will help:

- **You should create a letterhead giving your business name** and address and offer this to suppliers you contact by post or in person. This doesn't show how long you've been in business, thankfully, but it does prove you are serious and business-minded.

- **I've never ever had trouble obtaining goods from suppliers** and I have never had to prove myself for the purpose. You'll find many wholesale companies, operating online, will describe themselves clearly as 'Trade Only', meaning no one is allowed to buy individual products cheap for Christmas presents or personal use. The majority require you to open a trade account online, and in return for your contact details they'll give you a user name and password to access their 'secret, trade only' site. For 'Name', don't give your own name, give your business name instead, unless there's space for both. Do this even if you don't have a business bank account in that name. You do not need a business bank account to use a business name. Your eBay ID or Shop name will suffice so choose both with care.

- **You can trade under any name you like**, as long as you don't use the same or a similar name to already established companies with the intention of 'passing off' your business as part of theirs. Certain words are forbidden from trade names, such as 'Royal' and 'British' and numerous others you'll find listed in documents available from Companies House at www.companieshouse.gov.uk

- **When you meet suppliers**, by phone, mail, email, in person, refer to your business as a living entity. Say 'My firm is looking for widgets similar to those on your website', not 'My name's X Y and I wondered if you have anything I could sell'.

- **Remember what I said earlier and don't be side-tracked**: YOU ARE DOING THEM A FAVOUR BY SELLING THEIR PRODUCTS!!! If they don't understand that, move on!

Footnote

Read those last few paragraphs again about choosing your eBay ID with care. I chose 'boxersforever' for my eBay account, thinking how wonderful it sounded for dog-related items. Until someone asked me if I stocked Calvin Klein Boxer Shorts! Save yourself the embarrassment; when you find an ID or Shop name you like, ask friends and family what they think about it. Someone is bound to spot any problem you hadn't seen earlier.

Tips for buying at offline auctions

I have probably seen it all as far as auctions go and, though I've been buying at auction for more than thirty years, I still make mistakes, still find things to surprise me. This article is designed to help you avoid most of the problems typically encountered by newcomers and old hands alike.

- Visit as many auctions as you can to learn how individual auction companies operate. There are good, bad and downright ugly auction houses. All auction houses are bound by national and Statutory regulations, and all have their own independent rules detailing what they expect of bidders and buyers and what you can expect of them. Legally, national rules must be displayed somewhere prominent, in the auction catalogue, for example, or on a wall or notice board in the saleroom. Most companies combine national and company rules in one location. Read and make sure you understand what they mean and ask any questions before bidding.

- **Remember auction companies vary and what is common practice in one is entirely unsatisfactory in another**. Visit a few salerooms purely to view the proceedings and see how other visitors bid, how and where they collect their goods, and so on. Some companies allow goods to be taken during the sale, others don't. Some require payment on the day, others will wait ten days or more.

- **Following on from the last point, be careful about goods left in the saleroom while payment clears**. Typically, the auction company is not liable for the safety of your goods after the sale. If they get damaged, lost or stolen, that's your problem, not theirs. Try to pay on the day where possible and certainly in smaller auction houses and others best described as 'iffy'. Iffy, to my mind, describes

many non-custom built salerooms, such as auctions held in abattoirs and farm sales offices, any where porters are shabbily dressed, lack knowledge of individual lots, or just seem disinterested. Generally speaking, the best salerooms are those attached to large estate agencies and valuation specialists or with custom built auction rooms.

- **Arrive in plenty of time to get a really good look at anything you are interested in buying.** Inspect everything very carefully. Make sure items with multiple and moving parts are intact and working properly.

- **Be on your guard against popular cons, such as pieces from one lot being exchanged for bits from another,** after you have viewed and just before the auction begins. Be especially careful of large lots of collectibles, such as postcards and cigarette cards in albums or boxes, stamps, pieces of vintage jewellery, sets of toy soldiers. I've lost count of the number of times I've viewed postcards one day, bid and paid for them the next, and later discovered the real gems of the collection were missing. The cards have been moved to another box or album, originally containing low value cards which have been bought for next to nothing by the ruthless perpetrator. Check content before leaving and inform auction staff about irregularities. It's too late when you get home.

- **The 'panic button' is a popular con, whereby, as you are bidding**, probably against just one other person, someone will tap you on the shoulder and say something like: "Don't touch those ornaments, they're fakes". In the time it takes you to realise what's going on, some other person will have had the lot marked down to him. He and his friends have got what they wanted, in more ways than one!

- **Watch out for bids being 'taken off the wall',** involving non-existent bidders. This rarely happens in reputable auction houses, incidentally. Taking bids off the wall means what it says, and sometimes there is no-one bidding against you but the price keeps going up, and up. A dishonest auctioneer is reading your face to see just how far he can push you to bid. Confuse him, don't rush to bid, try to look as if you are losing interest at every bidding stage.

- **Remember that the price your lot is knocked down at can be inflated quite considerably by buyer's commission and statutory taxes**. Check before bidding and add likely extras to your maximum bidding budget.

- Remember you will have to get the things you buy to your home or business premises. Some auctions provide free transportation, many don't. If you have to hire a vehicle, take this into account when deciding how much to bid for certain lots.

- **Beware ex-demonstration goods;** they could be damaged. Look for fingerprints and stains indicating heavy use. Avoid stock other people have been unable to sell, they're not likely to sell for you either. Look especially for sticky patches where price labels have been removed. View goods from all angles and beat unscrupulous auctioneers' attempts to hide damaged goods by standing lots close to the wall, arranging items tightly together, placing doilies over heavy stains, painting over patched-up holes in cars and household goods.

- **Avoid items you can't try before bidding or risk buying computers that don't work**, televisions and radios minus essential components, books with pages missing.

WARNING! What you should never try listing on eBay

The swastika was once a sign of good luck; a symbol of hope and joy, good things for the future; it was also the emblem of the Finnish national airlines. And then came the dark days of World War Two.

List something emblazoned with a swastika – as I did an old good luck postcard – and you'll find it taken down with a stern warning from eBay.

How much better if I had taken a closer look at what is and what is not allowed to be sold on eBay and acted accordingly.

Banned Items include:

Nazi, Ku Klux Klan and murder-related memorabilia (wish I had known that sooner!)

Items with derogatory titles or descriptions. My

daughter had a listing removed for a print by Cecil Aldin of a dog with a name that today is a derogatory alternative to 'Negro'. Sad, but an easy mistake for one so young.

Credit Cards, Drugs and Drug Paraphernalia. Human Parts and Remains.

Some items, though not banned, are 'Questionable', such as:

Adults Only.
Plants and Seeds.
British Titles.
Food.

For a comprehensive list of barred, questionable and items potentially infringing copyright and trademark rules, go to:

http://pages.ebay.co.uk/help/sell/item_allowed.html

Selling strategies

Three main ways to sell

Surprisingly, not all eBay selling takes place by auction in the traditional sense of the word. There are in fact several selling methods, though for some you'll need to have a specific minimum feedback level and/or sign a Bank Debit agreement to pay eBay's fees.

The three main selling formats are:

Auction

This is the one most people are familiar with, where you list your item, state your opening bid price, choose whether to set a reserve, state how long the auction will run (1, 3, 5, 7, 10 days). It's also the main method for new eBayers who are not allowed to use BUY IT NOW until they have ten feedback points or agree to pay eBay fees by direct debit.

Buy It Now

This is where you state your price for the product, decide how many items to offer, and let people buy right away and pay by a variety of options. It's also the preferred method of virtually every PowerSeller, especially those favouring dropship selling. It works like a dream.

Shop

This is your shop on eBay, a place where you can list hundreds or thousands of Buy It Now items for as little as 6p per item payable every thirty days. Shop rental is £6 a month at basic level, more if you want a little extra exposure from eBay. I have found the basic level is adequate and there are many ways to publicise your shop yourself which cost absolutely nothing. I'll let you in on these ideas later. A minimum 20 feedback is required to open a shop.

A shop listing is particularly useful for anyone selling items within a common theme, such as doggy prints, as I do, which can feature in individual shop listings the likes of Poodle, Mastiff, Boxer, and so on.

In such a case an individual discovering your listing of rare prints of his or her favourite breed, will invariably visit your shop for a comprehensive listing of same breed items. At this stage he or she has almost forgotten about anyone else's listings on eBay and is focusing almost entirely on you.

Other

Other selling formats exist such as Private Auction and Dutch Auction which are worth learning about when you have experience of eBay in general. And of course we'll let you in on how to use them for maximum profit!

Why 'Auction' is often better than 'Shop' or 'Buy It Now' formats

- **Auction is the best way possible to 'price' an item whose value is uncertain** or for which guidelines are not available elsewhere. A good example is autographed items and signed letters from famous people no longer living. By their very nature many such items will have already been snapped up by collectors and the chance of new ones coming onto the market is far less than for similar items appearing from living celebrities!

- **Auction is a great way to test demand** for a product so you won't overstock on what later proves of no interest on eBay. Furthermore, early successful testing means you can buy in bulk and avoid running out of hot sellers. BUT: Be warned, just because a product is in fast demand today, doesn't mean it will sell well next month, or even next week. Other factors can reduce demand, such as changing consumer patterns, copycatting by rival suppliers, or the item may be a fad destined for limited shelf life. The moral is: don't ever buy more than you can realistically expect to sell!

- **Auction is also a good way to test the optimum price** for your product which, once ascertained, can be applied to BUY IT NOW and SHOP items.

Mystery auctions

Why Life Really is 'Like a Box of Chocolates – You Never Know What You're Gonna Get! Forrest Gump

Mystery Auctions are all the rage on eBay, especially in America, but catching on fast in the UK. As the name implies, bidders don't know exactly what they are going to get. A strange proposition, but very profitable for sellers, as you're about to discover.

I confess the whole thing seemed, still does seem like a scamsters' paradise to me, but eBay has created a specific category for Mystery Auctions and laid down rules by which sellers must abide. So they're happy to let them continue, for now.

Some weird items have been auctioned, such as a crumpled chewing gum wrapper minus gum, an empty box covered in dollar bills, a soiled and smelly nappy, an envelope containing some unspecified item. The 'unspecified' item is the real money spinner and can attract fierce bidding and incredibly high realisations.

The rules say there must be a product offered which people can see and eventually touch, like the empty box, the envelope, the chewing gum wrapper. Or the nappy!

This mystery product can be increased in value at specific bidding stages at which point sellers also typically give more clues to the identity of the mystery bonus. This is called a 'Progressive' Mystery Auction and it's potentially the most successful of all.

To learn more about mystery auctions, go to ebay.com, click on the 'Everything Else' category, go to 'Mystery Auctions'.

More than 1400 mystery auctions are currently listed on eBay.com, but as yet there is no special category in the UK, although a handful of mystery auctions can be found under 'Everything Else'.

Some big names exist in the Mystery Auction business, including philatelic suppliers, Stanley Gibbons, who regularly auction boxes containing stamps. The box is pictured, that's the product on offer, the stamps are the mystery bonus component.

A quick look at currently most watched mystery auctions will get your creative juices flowing.

• **There's a listing for something the seller has stuck in his pants** – it isn't a bubble gum wrapper, could it be a Porsche? The seller's words, not mine.

• **There's a box with something the seller bought for $5,000** dollars and decided not to give to his cheating wife.

• **A wife is selling an envelope containing her husband's pay cheques for the past six months.** A strange one this because it is the envelope that is for sale, the cheques are the gift, clues are given with each bid as to how much her husband actually made. How strange is that, the cheques have already been cashed, they're not transferable. Yet the listing is attracting lots of bids and will doubtless fetch a nice finishing price.

Strange and even stranger

If mystery auctions aren't strange enough, look at what also is currently listed for sale on eBay.com (and doubtless soon to be copied in the UK):

• **An apple shaped like a 'bum'.**

• **A chicken nugget shaped like a Seahorse.**

• **More than forty slices of toast are on sale, no doubt capitalising on a piece of toast containing an image of the Virgin Mary that sold for twenty eight thousand dollars.** You can even buy a 'Make Your Own Religious Toast Kit' from Christopher Curry, which regularly sells on eBay at $3,500 a time.

Visit 'Everything Else', then 'Weird Stuff', on eBay.com and prepare to be totally gob-smacked by the strangest things people are selling, and buying.

I am tempted to list a few mystery packages myself, but mine will be quality stuff, well worth the asking price, no empty dog food tins or used dentures from me.

Reverse auctions

eBay's 'Want It Now' format has one feature in common with genuine Reverse Auctions, namely that potential buyers post details of items they'd like to buy and wait for sellers to respond with suitable offers. But that's where the similarity ends because genuine reverse auctions have additional features:

• **In a reverse auction prices keep on going down, not up.**

• **Suppliers compete against one another by reducing their prices until no one is prepared to go lower.** That person is usually the winner and gets to sell his stock to the person who placed the ad.

• **Reverse auctions work much like items sold on tender where companies requiring goods or services invite offers from suppliers.** All things being equal the lowest bidder wins the contract. But unlike the tender system, with bids normally left in sealed envelopes until the offer deadline expires and each supplier can bid just once, in reverse auctions all bids are visible and suppliers can continue bidding against one another until the lowest price is achieved.

There is a downside to reverse auctions in that suppliers might get caught in a bidding frenzy in the same way buyers do in traditional auctions, and end up pricing themselves too low and actually losing money. The same could apply using eBay's 'Want It Now' feature, where it's common to see several seller responses and some sellers making regular repeat offers at lower prices to eventually win the sale.

Want It Now is a great way to find customers fast but like reverse auctions there are problems to contemplate.

Take your time with this new concept, study people placing and responding to posts, learn from their experience and incorporate this new medium slowly into your business.

A little knowledge goes a long way: Why eBay categories and country sites help you reach the highest profits

• **Generally speaking, items of international interest can generate bids from any country site**, unlike one-country specimens which are best placed on the actual or closest country option, alternatively on eBay.com for maximum audience potential. For example, a photograph of early French football teams I'd put on eBay.fr or eBay.com. An Australian team autographed cricket bat would go on eBay.com.au or eBay.com. I wouldn't list either on eBay.co.uk, and I'd never put Manchester United memorabilia anywhere but eBay.co.uk or eBay.com. For obvious reasons, if in doubt, choose eBay.com. You'll find most ardent sports collectors check by sports or celebrity name than by eBay category so most will find you wherever you list.

• **It's easy to list on eBay.com although you will have to create templates from scratch and price in dollars.** Check ££ values against their dollar equivalent at: www.xe.com/ucc/. Remember categories and some sports names differ between coun-

try sites, and be careful about postage and packing costs. My first listing on eBay.com was a disaster. I quite forgot that on eBay.com the UK is classed as overseas and America as local. All-in-all my offer of free domestic delivery and £5 for overseas fulfillment, meant everything I sent to America was postage free and UK buyers paid way over actual postage cost. I lost out big time on over 100 postcard listings.

• **Even if your listings vary little over several auction periods**, at least check what eBay category changes may have occurred to influence your chosen products. The completed listings feature is a great place to find highest recent realisations for products of the kind you are selling.

How to create profit-busting listings: It's not what you sell, it's the way that you sell it!

How you describe your goods is vitally important to your chances of making a little or a lot of money from every listing.

Your listing comprises not only words used in the title and body text; it includes layouts and colours, too, as well as fonts, size of text, even the length of sentences and paragraphs. These tips will help you list more products, create better listings and eventually make more money:

• **Inside your listing, give viewers a reason to call back later** if they are in a hurry now or not quite ready to bid. Ask them to visit your 'About Me' page for a free eBook or newsletter and be sure they give their email addresses for you to contact them later. You can also begin a mailing list for later sales outside of eBay. Remind them, too, to add you to their Favourite Sellers list.

• **Choose keywords to describe your items and use them in the heading and body of your listings.** People can choose to search according to heading (title) or by checking body text too, but few remember to check the box to include this second option. Most people will find your product by either going directly to category listings and clicking through to their appropriate sub-category or, most likely, by simply keying words to describe the item into eBay's search tool. This means if your title does not include those keywords your listing will be missed. Check what keywords are most common when people search for items like those you are listing by going to http://pulse.ebay.co.uk (or .com or other) and continue through the sub-categories until your product type appears. Now check the most commonly keyed search terms at the left of the screen. Alternatively, go to 'Advanced Search', top right of screen and on the next page use keywords to describe your item and tick the 'Completed Auctions' box. From the results choose 'Price: Highest First' to locate similar items, check the keywords used in the heading on which to model your own. Be careful not to breach eBay's stringent rules on 'Keyword Spamming'.

- **Avoid using too many bells and whistles in your listings.** One that is guaranteed to make me move away really fast is the wizard that flits about the screen thanking me for visiting and generally getting in the way of everything I am trying to see. Music, flashing lights, moving conveyor belt pictures of other products from which to choose a selection – if you're quick enough – have roughly the same effect, as do many other totally useless and generally hugely frustrating devices.

- **Use colour, sparingly**, in your listings, as well as experimenting with different fonts and font sizes. It all adds interest for the visitor while also creating a professional image for your business.

- **Never write titles in full upper case** – CAPITALS. IT LOOKS AWFUL, UNPROFESSIONAL, AND FAR FROM ATTRACTING ATTENTION IT MAKES YOUR TITLE MUCH HARDER TO READ. IT IS OKAY TO USE UPPER CASE ON ONE OR TWO WORDS IN YOUR TITLE.

- **Try using html to create a more professional appearance especially in highly competitive product fields.** For old postcards and other rare, sometimes one-off collectibles, basic text is fine. Where similar or identical items are available from numerous sellers, such as CDs, modern jewellery, make up, improving the appearance of your listing will help distinguish your business from others with hastily created listings packed with spelling mistakes, poor descriptions, and so on.

- **Basic html is very easy to use and stunning auc-tion templates can be created in Microsoft Word or FrontPage**. Alternatively, choose from thousands of free and low-cost auction templates available online.

- **Use templates where possible**, it saves listing time later, and can create a more professional appearance. They can look especially good with subtle use of colours, different fonts, background designs; subtle meaning delicate, not garish or gaudy. In future issues we will include news of free to download templates for our subscribers only.

- **Use fonts that make reading easy**. Never make it too hard for visitors to read your listing or they will do the most intelligent thing. Click out and look somewhere else to buy! Most popular fonts are Times, Times Roman, Arial, New York, Verdana.

- **When you find a font you like**, stick with it, don't change fonts between templates. It isn't worth it and time wasted would be better spent on listing new items. Avoid using too much italic or other embellishing devices such as embossing or shadowing in your listings.

- **Do not use large fonts in your listings**, except for headings and sub-headings, and even those do not need to be more than two or three sizes bigger than body text. Size 12 or 14 is adequate for body text, 18 for main headings, 16 for sub-headings.

- **Very large text is a big put-off and is also difficult to read**, while also absorbing more memory and taking longer to upload and download.

- **Use a maximum two or three different colour fonts** (including basic black or navy or other appropriate choice) and never use different colours within the same word. I know major companies like eBay do it but they are well-known, their logos are professionally created, anything less would look trashy and cheap. Not to mention hugely unprofessional.

- **Keep text aligned to the left**, sometimes to the right where the graphic is placed extreme left. Don't centre or justify a column of text without good reason. And there are few if any goods reasons for doing so. Centred text is difficult to read and creates odd lengths that create a totally amateurish appearance. Justified text is even worse with lengthy gaps between words which themselves are longer than average.

• **Keep listings fairly narrow especially when using html**. Wide listings are okay on wide screen computers, but on narrow screen computers the entire right side will be missing and few people will scroll left and right every few seconds to get the gist of your listing. eBay's own listing boxes, that is where you type directly into eBay, and those created in *Turbo Lister*, are just the right size, never too long, never too short. When using html or creating your own designer template, practice using eBay's systems first to get the desired length.

• **Keep paragraphs short and always with a gap between them**. And actually USE PARAGRAPHS where text extends beyond two or three lines. Notice how some listings containing hundreds, sometimes thousands of words, are created in one L – O – N – G chunk which no one in their right mind would read. Others with long, long descriptions actually use paragraphs though the effect is hardly noticeable.

• **Try to stagger listings even if you list just once a week**. This helps people who are bidding on several of your items and might want to check last minute bidding against them on those items. Too many of their chosen items ending within seconds of each other is confusing and frustrating for them, and means you lose out on last minute impulse bids. Using *Turbo Lister* you can choose how many already listed items to upload at any time, say in units of 20, and you can also alter the order of items to hopefully prevent 'same item' products selling within seconds of each other.

How to list your items faster

• **Try listing and uploading items directly into eBay to learn the ropes.** Then move on to using specialist listing software like *Turbo Lister* which lets you create and store templates as well as allowing you to list as many items as required before uploading to eBay. Some sellers, for example, list items daily, often directly into eBay. This means you'll always have something selling but also creates problems of packing and posting almost daily. Others prefer to upload once a week, say on Sunday evening, so when an auction ends, the following Sunday evening, they can send invoices last thing at

night in preparation for posting paid for items the next day alongside listing new items to upload the following Sunday. This latter option works very well and means posting and packing can be done largely in one fell swoop with just minor jobs left over for late payers, second chance sales, and so on. *Turbo Lister* is free and can be downloaded from eBay's 'Seller Services' section.

• **Use *Turbo Lister* to create lots of templates for similar or identical items,** such as all maps and prints from one book, all CDs by a particular artist, all salt and pepper shakers bought at recent boot sales, and so on.

• **Be very careful using *Turbo Lister* and the relisting option in your eBay account.** It is very, very easy to duplicate an item unintentionally, only to discover later it was the wrong item or a time-sensitive mention in the listing makes it appear ridiculous and you look a total plonker. As an example, I had clock cufflinks that were selling like a dream, which I kept on relisting, and which eventually stopped selling almost overnight. When I checked, months after the original listing was created, I discovered 'Great Valentine's Day Gift' still appearing in the listing was putting people off in the run up to Christmas!!!!

Low-cost, no-cost ways to get buyers into your eBay Shop

Shop listings cost a tiny fraction of promoting your products by auction or Buy It Now. But there's a catch, unless you pay more to promote your shop, your listings don't show in normal search results.

So you could be wasting money rather than saving it unless you work at promoting your shop listings.

These are simple solutions, ways to make your shop listings jump out and get noticed; it's all so easy, cheap, and takes just a little time and energy.

Let's say you are selling a line of related products, such as fishing lures, dog breed mugs, sports theme cufflinks, and so on. Your options are to list potentially hundreds of items Buy It Now or Auction, with relatively high costs compared to listing items in your eBay shop for just a few pennies per item each month.

But without appearing in search listings, how do you get people interested in fishing lures, dog breed mugs, sports theme cufflinks, to visit your shop?

These ideas will help.

USING SUB-TITLES IN NORMAL AUCTION LISTINGS

Auction listings like these help promote hundreds of other items. Notice how the sub-title, costing 35 pence a time highlights other items available in the seller's eBay shop.

DIVING CUFFLINKS, PEWTER, CRAFTSMAN MADE, QUALITY
Many More Sports Theme Cufflinks in our eBay Store

FISHING LURE ~ **NEW** ~ PSYCHADELIC COLOURS
Visit Our eBay Shop for ALL Your Fishing Needs

TEA TIME WITH YOUR DOG ~ CERAMIC MUG
100 + Different Breed Mugs in Our eBay Shop

Notice:

1) The cufflinks listing mentions other sports theme cufflinks available in store. But, depending on its chosen category, this might not be a good advertisement. Sports items have their own eBay category, so cricket cufflinks can go in the Sports>Cricket section, tennis into Sports>Tennis, and so on. It's rather pointless highlighting other sports themes to people who are interested in cricket and nothing but cricket. But under the general cufflinks category – Jewellery>Men's Jewellery>Cufflinks – a sub-heading mentioning other sports – subject to conditions regarding keyword spamming – will work very well. The question is, which sport gets used as your lead listing? I recommend you choose a high profile, all-year-round sport like cricket or football, as opposed to a minority sport like kitesurfing. We're looking for maximum exposure, that's all, not necessarily a sale.

2) The fishing lure advertisement uses the lure to draw attention to lots of other items the fisherman will find in the advertiser's eBay shop: rods, boating trips, protective clothing, reels, and so much more. It might be considered keyword spamming to actually name specific items in the title or sub-title but there is nothing to prevent you using a generic mention of other products on offer. The same goes for the sports and dog breed listing titles shown earlier, where the sub-heading is generic, not keyword spamming, unlike for instance the next headlines which names specific sports and dog breeds. **The following two examples are not acceptable to eBay and would be removed and could get you expelled.**

DIVING CUFFLINKS, PEWTER, CRAFTSMAN MADE, QUALITY
Soccer, Fishing, Shooting, Golf, Cricket Cufflinks in our eBay Store

TEA TIME WITH YOUR DOG ~ CERAMIC MUG
Akita, Boxer, Bulldog, Pomeranian, Pug, Spaniel + 100s More in our eBay Shop

3) Don't use Buy It Now for this system. You are aiming for a long lasting listing, not necessarily to eventually sell your item. The intention is to draw attention to your shop for as long as possible. For the same reason it makes sense to use ten day auctions rather than shorter listings.

Using loss leaders in normal auction listings

You could price your auction item very low with the intention of getting people to enter your listing to place a bid. This is called a 'loss leader' and it means you risk losing money on one product in order to generate more sales of other products later. Once people are attracted inside your low bid price listing you can redirect them to your shop or About Me page for more information about shop products.

This is how I might promote shop listings of those doggy cufflinks I'm always talking about.

DOG BREED CUFFLINKS

Gold Plated, Fabulous Detail, 1p Starting Price,
No Reserve

I don't mention the specific breed in the title, and I don't use a tell-tale gallery picture either. Both techniques help raise curiosity and attract people inside my listing. Once inside, they will see the picture, it may not be their favourite breed, but right alongside they'll see that 100 plus more breeds are available in my eBay shop.

I am aware that my sample title includes way too many characters, but the point is to reveal ways to get people into my listing out of pure curiosity and maybe to bid. I could do without my item selling at this low price, but if that is what it takes to generate multiple sales of cufflinks inside my store, that's fine by me.

A great many people will go into the listing to bid on the chance of getting something valuable for just one penny, some will leave without bidding, others will visit my shop and buy.

Had I used a graphic it would be of a little known, not easily identifiable breed, rather than an obvious Poodle or Pug. My aim would be to get people into the listing to learn what this unfamiliar breed is. Remember you can't mention other breeds in the listing, that could be classed as keyword spamming (read more about this later), but inside your shop you are allowed to create a type of promotional banner which lists categories that show through to all of your listings. So on that listing for Boxer Dog Cufflinks, though I can't add 'Akita, Alsatian' and such to my actual title or listings, I can create shop categories called 'Akita Cufflinks' and 'Alsatian Cufflinks' that will appear inside all of my listings. Of course this is only possible if you actually have an eBay shop.

Use keyword rich descriptions

A good listing is one that shows up whenever someone searches for products similar to those you are selling. eBay's most successful sellers work hard to predict virtually any word or phrase a potential customer might use in their search, only then can they be absolutely sure their listing doesn't get lost among masses of competing products.

The secret is to include in all your titles, sub-titles and listings, all the relevant key words and phrases potential bidders might use to find products like yours. By 'relevant', I mean words that actually apply to your specific product, not to similar items available elsewhere in your listings. That is keyword spamming.

'Keyword Rich' is the term to describe a listing containing many of the most relevant words and phrases likely to be used by potential buyers for a specific product.

It's worth spending time creating your listing, especially for high profit repeat sale products. Get the first listing right and the product can run with just a few essential checks later.

There are ways to check keywords people use on eBay, such as by looking on the Pulse pages, but my preferred way it through www.overture.com. I reckon people using overture to search for products outside of eBay are using much the same words and phrases as their eBay buying counterparts, but that's just my opinion.

Copy me by going to www.overture.com where you'll find the worldwide search terms category by clicking on 'Visit the Resource Center' and then on 'Keyword Selector Tool'. On Overture's front page you can locate keyword search words and phrases for specific countries by choosing the appropriate country flag top right of the screen and going through a similar progress as just described.

Key in words to describe your product, such as 'mobile phone', 'masonic', 'cat', and so on. Let your imagination roam free, remember a phone is also a telephone, a Mason is also a Freemason, a cat can also be a Siamese or a Moggy. Keep Overture's lists of most commonly used keywords and phrases, especially the first fifty or so, from the highest down to lowest frequency search terms. Underlined words and phrases can be clicked on and opened to reveal more searches containing those particular words. When you're describing your product, include as many relevant words as possible, especially those higher up the list, but avoid keyword spamming.

Rebate programmes and the very best advertising money really can't buy

Looking much like a typical supermarket loyalty programme where goods are discounted according to points awarded from past spends, some innovative eBay sellers have started offering rebates to their customers. One of the most novel schemes was started by Brian Cohen who calls his rebate program 'a conceptual art project in the form an interactive rebate'. He even created a website for the program at (http://www.showmebay.com)

Enthusiasts say that rebate programs create visibility for their auctions and help customers bring the seller quickly to mind and generate additional sales over an indefinite period.

The rebate sale has other benefits too, especially those that work on the basis of buyers sending photographs showing them using the product.

You've seen newspaper promotions packed with before and after pictures and others showing everyday folk enjoying a product. They're very persuasive but are often viewed with suspicion and the subject of many investigations by government and trade consumer organisations. In short, there's often little to prove the photographs are genuine or an illusion of over-enthusiastic copywriters.

Cohen and others like him invite customers to send pictures of a product being used which are uploaded to eBay with the subject's ID included together with recommendations and testimonials. "People naturally feel more comfortable using a product if they see other people using the same product", Cohen told US editors, "Moreover, the pictures would act as models or digital mannequins for my merchandise for future bidders to see".

It also gives people something to talk about, something to tell their friends, and can lead to many more people viewing your listings than might otherwise be so.

A neat piece of marketing, one you might consider for your business.

At www.showmebay.com Cohen says: "The Winning bidder receives a 50% rebate if they send us within 3 Weeks of delivery of qualified items (qualified items are listed as a "ShowMe! Rebate") a picture of the recipient wearing the winning bid item bought from Bidofthis.com on eBay! To qualify you must indicate within 24 hours of actual purchase that you are qualifying for the Bidofthis.com ShowMe! Rebate."

It's important to specify that all pictures become your copyright and that they may be used to promote your product on and outside of eBay.

This is how to integrate this great idea into your business:

1) Read and follow eBay's rules regarding free gifts and competitions. Learn more at: http://pages.ebay.co.uk/help/policies/listing-bonus-prize-giveaway-raffle.html

2) Decide how the rebate can benefit you apart from generating more bidding interest. Are you wanting testimonials, or pictures, a name on your mailing list, something else?

3) Work out how best to accomplish your objective via a rebate scheme. You could for example add a note saying that anyone sending a picture of themselves wearing your training shoes will qualify for the rebate. Emphasise you may use the photographs in other promotions.

4) Decide how much you can afford to give back to your customer. Remember you only need a few great pictures or testimonials to make it work in your favour.

5) Give specific details of who qualifies and how, when and by what method the rebate is given, if any specific conditions apply.

6) Ask for payment by PayPal, where refunding is fast and straightforward and provides a permanent record of the transaction taking place. Do not include postage and packing in the refund price, give the rebate purely on the selling price of the product.

7) Don't worry, you are not about to wash half your profits down the drain every day. You can termi-

nate the program any time you like although you must not terminate a listing offering a rebate which has bids. That is dishonest, and illegal, and will earn you well deserved negative feedback. The even better news is, the *Wall Street Journal* reports that bidding typically goes far higher with the rebate than without even though less than 5 per cent of people actually claim a rebate. It seems most people forget about the rebate, many can't be bothered to claim, some lose their rebate details, others get preoccupied and run out of time for the rebate.

Don't rest on the Sabbath day – that's when the really big money is made

The weekend, notably Sunday, Saturday to a lesser extent, when more people are off work and using their computers, is the best time to end an auction in expectation of high visitor levels and greater chance of a bidding frenzy for your listings.

We find Sunday evening, 6 pm onwards, is the optimum time for us and many other prolific sellers.

So, for a seven day listing, surely that means spending all weekend photographing and describing items to sell seven days hence? While other people are off work?

Not so, you can in fact work just a few days, Sunday not included, and still have all sales end Sunday at a precise time that suits you best.

This is how:

• Using *Turbo Lister* you can list as many items as you wish and upload to eBay at leisure, in this case round about 6pm on Sunday evening. Obviously, the more items uploaded this way, the longer it takes, and you might find uploading one thousand items, starting 6pm takes you way beyond next week's 6pm sale ending deadline. First week is unpredictable, next week start uploading earlier to meet that 6pm deadline.

• Use 3, 5, 7 or 10 day auctions according to days you list items. So if you're listing Saturday and Sunday, use 7 day auctions, they'll end next weekend. Monday and Tuesday use 5 day auctions, again ending Saturday or Sunday. Wednesday and Thursday use 3* or 10 days auctions, again for weekend finishes. Fridays don't fit the plan, and one day auctions are generally too short for all but perishable and really hot selling items. *Three day auctions aren't always a good idea either, so test carefully, or use ten day listing instead.

• The biggest bonus of all listings ending together is that you can plan your week more profitably, visiting auctions, checking suppliers, fulfilling orders, without having to be home every day answering last minute questions from last minute bidders.

Creating eBooks to market your eBay products or even for selling the book itself on eBay

Our readers are fascinated by the hugely profitable prospect of marketing eBooks on eBay, but sometimes lack knowledge for turning their book into digital format, ready for uploading or fulfilling as an attachment or on CD.

In this excerpt from a longer article you can finish reading on our site – www.1st-in-auctions.com/louis.html – veteran Internet marketer, writer and publisher, Louis Allport helps you choose formats for your product, explaining the pros and cons and helping our readers better understand the possibility of formatting eBooks purely as a means of selling other products on eBay.

Know about "Viral eBooks"?

by Louis Allport

It's not a new concept I'll admit, but it works like absolute gangbusters. In fact, over the past three years it has personally been responsible for bringing me hundreds of thousands of visitors to just one of my websites. AND – 100% for free.

Getting traffic with Viral eBooks is a 'free traffic tactic', which means you're not paying for advertising. But, because you're not paying for this exposure, you need to instead create content that people WANT to pass on.

This takes effort, but if you do it right, it can pay you back hugely. Let's go through it:

Okay – for starters you can create Viral eBooks in two formats:

1) EXE (executable) format – which means it only works on PCs. This type of eBook looks like a website packaged together.

These types of eBooks look great, and all someone has to do to view it is download and double-click it. But, as mentioned it does only work on PCs, and generally the software to create these types of eBooks isn't free, although it is very affordable.

2) Alternatively – you can create and distribute Viral eBooks in the hugely popular PDF format. The advantage of PDF is that everyone can read them successfully whether they're viewing your eBook on PC, Mac or 'other'.

To read PDF successfully, the person who downloaded the eBook needs to have the free Adobe Reader installed on their computer. Most people do, and if they don't it's a quick download from Adobe.com, so this isn't an issue.

Although PDFs can be more widely read that EXE style eBooks, they're not quite as flexible. With EXEs for example you can actually embed video and audio into the eBook. This isn't possible with PDF. With PDF you would need to instead include a link to where the reader can view or download the audio/video online.

So with this in mind, you need to decide what's most important to you and make your choice accordingly for eBook format. I personally don't recommended you create your eBook in both formats, since that just complicates the distribution process in my experience. Stick with one or the other.

For creating viral PDFs – there's a wide array of software you can use. Some of this software is free, some mind-bogglingly expensive. To view many available options, simply search Download.com or Tucows.com.

For creating viral PDFs, I personally use software that I had specially created. And the advantage of my software is that it allows you to easily create fully 'brandable' PDFs. This means that people can customize your PDF with their own affiliate or website details.

The benefit of this feature is that it makes it much more likely the PDF will spread far and wide for you as it gives the reader a strong incentive to pass the PDF on as they can now directly profit from its distribution.

Louis Allport is an online product developer and marketer. To get a free download of his powerful "Viral PDF Generator" software, visit www.BrandPDF.com

Ten things that might mean your item is valuable

When is a book not a book? When it's autographed, for example, or in pristine condition despite being centuries old, and other factors that make it stand out from the crowd.

These are a few of many reasons an item – not just books by the way – may be worth nothing and another virtually priceless:

• **Is it dated?** Dated items are usually provenance proved, not subject to guesswork. But, consider: is it original or a reproduction or reprint? Be careful, if it's dated, give the date, but don't testify to age. For example, a book dated 1900 may indeed have been printed that year, and be 105 years old, or it could be a modern reprint. If you're unsure you could say: 'Dated 1900, in good condition', but not 'Dated 1900. A wonderful example at 105 years old'. Play it safe and on all your listings add: 'All items described to the best of our knowledge and ability'. A satisfaction or money back guarantee also protects you against problems of innocently mis-describing items.

• **Is there a signature?** Did this otherwise ordinary item have a famous owner to increase its value? Is the signature genuine? Or a forgery? Is the signature original or printed onto the item? If the signature is original, is it the hand of the famous person or an agent charged with signing on their behalf?

- **Is it in good condition?** Do you understand what 'good condition' means for this particular item? Many collectibles, such as books, postcards, stamps, have industry recognised grading standards to which you should also conform. For example, unused collectors' stamps with hinge marks, are not mint, but can be described as unused or mounted, and other recognised descriptions.

- **Is it rare?** Or is it something quite common but new to you? What does rare really mean? Unless you are sure, describe it as 'unusual' or 'uncommon', not rare.

- **It is antique?** So many things described as antique are simply old, less than one hundred years to which the word antique really applies. So say 'old' or 'vintage', not 'antique', unless you're sure of that 100 year rule.

- **Was the item designed for heavy use, such as pots and pans, coins and banknotes, and unlikely to survive the decades intact?** Was the item ephemeral, of limited shelf life, such as theatre tickets, newspapers, and typically used or given away in hours or days? If the item has survived decades, intact, it could be valuable, maybe very valuable.

- **Does the item have 'double appeal'?** Might it attract bids from two or more different eBay categories and consequently multiple bids, such as a book on a popular theme, but a collectible author, with a famous previous owner. A plate I bought at the auction of Dame Catherine Cookson's effects presented four collecting themes: as a plate in its own right (very popular collecting area), famous owner (well-known novelist), Ringtons design (advertising), area of manufacture (Newcastle-on-Tyne). Oh yes, it was also blue and white, another major collecting interest.

- **Is the price too low for comfort?** Is it a fake or reproduction? Broken? Even worse, stolen? Check items thoroughly, ask for proof of previous ownership, buy from reputable sellers only, avoid itinerant sellers at flea markets and boot sales unless they provide receipts and contact details. Most boot sale and flea market sellers are very genuine and a majority of organisers now provide written details of traders at the event. Stolen items belong to their

original owner, not the innocent buyer.

How to save on listing fees

It costs just 75p to list an item on eBay UK starting price £29.99 or less. Invite bids of £30.00 or and you'll pay £1.50 up to maximum £99.99 starting price.

Unsurprisingly, new sellers, more keen to get their listings online fast than check listing fees first, opt for a 'nice round figure' to start with, £30 for instance, rather than £29.99. I know that for a fact, because I did it myself, so did my daughters, not one of us realised the extra penny on starting price set us back a massive 75p.

Effectively, we could have, indeed we now do, prefer to list two items starting price £29.99 which costs exactly the same as another item starting price £30 and not guaranteed to sell.

We're just talking starting prices here, not final realisations, and if you're product's worth thirty pounds plus, other things can be done to protect your profits and finishing price. Set a reserve for example. Or offer second chance offers, do Dutch Auctions, do Buy It Now with multiple listings, where duplicate products are plentiful and readily available. We'll tell you how to do this in a forthcoming issue, but for now it pays to understand how eBay's fees work.

Study the current listing fees for eBay UK and decide whether asking a penny more is really worthwhile based on likely final value of your product and optional cost of setting a reserve price. You'll find them at: http://pages.ebay.co.uk/help/sell/fees.html

These are the current listing fees, sometimes called 'Insertion Fees'.

Starting Price	Fee
£0.01 to 0.99	15p
£1.00 tp £4.99	20p
£5.00 to £14.99	35p
£15.00 to £29.99	75p
£30.00 to £99.99	£1.50
£100.00 and Up	£2.00

So, a listing for item starting price £4.99 with

gallery picture is 35p, start a penny higher and pay 50p, (add £60 reserve and price is £2.85 whether your starting price is £4.99 or £5.00 but that's another story). It sounds confusing, in practice it can be very confusing, but with a pen and paper at hand it's well worth recording prices for all the listing options of a popular or rare product.

Here's a great idea. *Turbo Lister* is eBay's free bulk listing programme, it can be used to store regular listings, keep records of one-off unrepeatable listings, and it is a great way to calculate fees much faster than by testing directly through eBay's main site.

Go to: http://pages.ebay.co.uk/turbo_lister/index.html to learn more about and download *Turbo Lister*.

You don't have to actually use *Turbo Lister* to benefit from its help in pricing your listings. You install *Turbo Lister* on your computer following the easy instructions involved. Now list an item, don't worry, it's very easy, and worth doing even if just for price testing purposes. Press the 'Add To Upload' button, click the arrow top right, then go into the uploading section top of the Turbo Lister screen.

This is how to test other starting prices for your test listing. Click on the listing to open, notice top right there are boxes for starting price, buy it now price, reserve price. Enter figures in one or more of those boxes, based on how many items you have to sell, what is your minimum selling price, how much you'd really like to achieve if a reserve is set. Save your findings. Now – CAREFULLY – press the 'upload all to eBay' button. You can choose to upload specific items or all together which is easy to learn but for now we're testing prices and you'll see when you pressed the button that *Turbo Lister* began checking listing fees for your item. When the price appears, make a written note of price, then press 'Cancel'. ***Press 'Continue' and your listing will be uploaded to eBay warts and all – Not Recommended.*** Now make other changes to starting, buy it now, reserve prices, follow the test upload procedure again, notice the difference in listing fees. Do this with all listings for potentially valuable and all repeat product listings and achieve the very best returns for your advertising budget.

Note that the maximum insertion fee for any Multiple Item Listing and all individual items starting price £100 or over is £2.00, excluding real estate and motors and some other exceptions.

If I walked in the room naked – would you notice me then?

That made you take notice, as well it should.

The same goes for auction titles which must also grab the attention, arouse curiosity, sometimes shock, and ultimately sell!

With the 'right' title, the most ordinary product can attract hundreds of views, and bidders, too.

The following advice from eBay seller and writer Ben Catt will help you create great titles.

How to write a traffic pulling eBay auction title

by Ben Catt

Selling an item on eBay should be simple but it is surprising how many people make some very silly mistakes.

As a buyer this is fantastic, you can pick up some absolute bargains by finding poorly listed items. However, if you are a seller you need to ensure that every item you put on eBay will be found and therefore have a better chance of commanding a high price.

Your auction title is really the most important part of your auction, after all, it is this feature which attracts buyers to view your description.

You have 55 characters to use to attract the bidders, try and use all of them – it is free and the more relevant keywords you can add, the more search results your auction will end up in.

For example:

A listing with the title: **"Band of Brothers Region 2 – 6 DVDs – UK Version – Mint"** is likely to receive a great deal more interest than one with the following title: **"band of brothers dvd"**

Also, try and avoid writing the entire title in capitals or using unrelated words like "L@@K" and "W@W". This simply annoys other eBay users and is not good netiquette.

Never keyword spam either. You see this all of the time on eBay, sellers add unrelated keywords to the title so their auction lands in more search results.

The problem is that these keywords won't attract more bids but simply attract users who are searching for something else entirely.

If you list an auction for a Playstation 2 but use the title **"Playstation 2 not Xbox not Nintendo"** it will attract people who are not looking for a Playstation 2. Quite simply, people who are not looking for a PS2 will not buy one.

Your time would be better served adding more relevant keywords to the title. **"Sony Playstation 2 (PS2) – Mint in Box – No Reserve"** is a much better title.

Where possible, try and include descriptive keywords to attract bidders. Some good examples are the following:

Rare, Mint, OOP (Out of Print), Low P&P, No Reserve or NR, Low Starting Price, 1p Starting Bid, Brand New etc.

Ensure you spellcheck your title before you list it. This is easy to do if you write the title in *Microsoft Word* first. If you spell an important keyword incorrectly you will miss out on a lot of potential bidders.

To make the title look more attractive, add a capital to the front of every major keyword.

"Microsoft Xbox – Mint in Box with 4 Games – No Reserve"

looks more attractive and stands out more than:

"microsoft xbox – mint in box with 4 games – no reserve"

If you are unsure of the best way to write your title, try searching for the same item under Completed Listings and see how others have done it before.

If their auctions have commanded high winning bids then their titles have worked.

Don't be afraid to copy them. (**Editor:** But not too closely or you might risk breaking copyright, plagiarism, or even trademark laws).

Ben Catt is an active eBay seller and owner of an eBay Tips and Tricks site found at http://bencatt.com

How to upload pictures to your listings

Pictures are the first thing most people see of your products, they must look good or your listing won't be opened.

However, there are times when having no gallery picture actually works better than having one, such as for postcards and other collectibles where just one word triggers interest in the subject, with or without a picture alongside.

So someone collecting postcards of, say, Crimdon in County Durham, will click on every listing having Crimdon in the title, even without a gallery picture.

This doesn't work for most listings, a picture really does sell products, and the picture has to be good.

Uploading pictures is one of the most commonly experienced early problems of new eBayers, so let's go with a few tips to help you create wonderful images of your products that encourage people to buy, buy, buy.

Firstly, although many image formats work well, I personally prefer jpeg. Using a scanner or digital camera, jpeg is one of the saving options, alongside various others.

Let's go with jpeg, and once our images are scanned or processed on digital camera, we'll save them on the desktop in jpeg format, preferably in a specially named folder.

Now go through the normal process of listing items for sale on eBay, starting with choosing a category, producing a title, and listing, then on to 'Pictures and Item Details' where you give starting price, length of auction, and pictures.

You can choose between uploading pictures to your own Internet space, or use eBay's hosting service. I know how to upload pictures to my own space but I actually like using eBay so you might do the same until you gain experience.

At the point on the 'Pictures and Item Details'

page where it says 'Add Pictures and Gallery', go to the line entitled 'Picture 1' and then click on 'Browse'. A new box will open with another entitled 'Look In' at the far top. At the menu right side of 'Look In', choose 'Desktop', that's where we stored the folder containing our pictures. Next highlight your pictures folder and press 'Open'. Look for and highlight the graphic you require and again click 'Open'. The graphic's title should now appear in box 'Picture 1' on the 'Picture and Item Details' page.

Further down tick 'Gallery' if you want the picture to appear outside your listing where it will show among all other listings in your chosen category. Scroll down and press 'Continue'.

That's it, all done.

How to start a bidding war

Imagine Just Two People in the Whole Wide World Want Something You Are Selling... Just Two People... Now Imagine More than Two People, Many More... Imagine Fierce Fighting Where You Are the Eventual Winner

A bidding war is where two or more people bid furiously against one another, each desperate to own a particular item.

Phenomenal results are possible, such as last month, where a postcard by artist A. R. Quinton, depicting a cliff view at Herne Bay, fetched £100 plus. By anyone's standards, the card was worth about £3 for the view and maybe a few pounds more for the artist.

I checked and found that two serious bidders, one of Herne Bay topographical postcards, the other a Quinton enthusiast, had launched a bidding war that was eventually won by the Herne Bay collector, or was it the seller of this rather common-a-garden postcard?

Such events are not uncommon. My own best selling item this month, a pair of vintage cufflinks with ancient Greek Coins, for which I paid £3 at a flea market, went for £34, with the two final bidders being a collector of cufflinks and another of Greek coins. The Greek coin collector won.

You only need two bidders and it doesn't matter if they're interested in the same product or specific parts of your product or listing. The end result is always the same; more money for you.

You're looking for just two people in the whole wide world, these tips will help you find them.

- **List a minimum two items (or themes) in one lot.** The trick is to make each item valuable in its own right and appealing to more than one person. The cufflinks and postcard are good examples. I've seen other wars raging over two completely unrelated postcards listed together; two books bearing no relation to one another; a pack of artist illustrated playing cards where one bidder wanted the cards and the other collected all things artist related.

- **List in two eBay categories to achieve maximum market penetration.** You can also list in two shop categories. For the Quinton/Herne Bay postcard I'd list under 'Artist Drawn Postcards' and 'Topographical'.

- **Research and use commonly used keywords** for your product to attract the highest audience for your item. Go to eBay Pulse pages for common keywords or use software such as *Adword Analyzer* to study most commonly used key words and phrases for specific subjects. Although developed largely for search engine optimisation and Google advertising campaigns and similar, products like *Adword Analyzer* are equally suitable for all areas of the Internet, including eBay. Visit our site, www.1st-in-auctions.com/Keywords.html for more ideas on keyword research with tips from top eBayers and other Internet marketers.

- **Offer free gifts and bonuses to attract interest from people selling similar items.** For example, offer three cufflinks where most offer two (emphasise these things get damaged, lost, stolen); ship items postage free; add complementary items such as matching tie pin (free or otherwise) with cufflinks, free presentation boxes with every batch of wholesale necklaces, and so on.

- **Offer a free gift that is valuable in its own right, worth more than the product listed, and not available from any other source.** Remember to change the freebie regularly as frequent buyers will have it already. Study and comply with eBay rules regarding gifts, bonuses and discounts. The trick is to find people not necessarily wanting your listed product, but very keen on the freebie. Learn more at: http://pages.ebay.co.uk/help/policies/listing-bonuses.html

How one short email can sell thousands of pounds worth of your products

Many eBay PowerSellers issue newsletters, sometimes called ezines – normally by email – to their customers as a means of generating repeat business for their products. This additional business, usually outside of eBay, has zero selling costs, needs just an Internet connection and takes just a few hours each month. The results are spectacular, often exceeding eBay sales.

The reason:

• **People who've bought from you once and enjoyed the experience** are more likely to buy from you again, perhaps over the lifetime of your mutual existence.

• **New customers are much harder to find**, and more expensive to reach, than past buyers whose details you already have.

• **It costs little or nothing to email past buyers** with hundreds of current offers unlike listing those hundreds of items individually on eBay.

• **Competition is zero**, you have a target audience of people who trust you, people whose buying habits you understand and can use to source products entirely suited to them.

• **You can even test how often your customers buy**, how much they spend, which times of year fetch higher sales, which incentives work best, and more. This means you can categorise customers as regular buyers – worth mailing several times a month; seasonal buyers – email at Christmas, Easter, etc.; one-time only – they bought once, haven't bought for a year, probably time to delete them from your mailing list.

It's easy to collect emails from people who've purchased already, but what of those who visited your listing and didn't bid, and others who did bid but weren't the eventual winner? How do you get them onto your mailing list? Very easy, you ask them to join!

Copy this simple message I use in my listings for resell rights products:

'Visit my About Me page for free weekly tips to help you build a profitable business selling ebooks and resell rights products'.

That simple statement can be amended to suit most products. For example:

'Visit my About Me page for free weekly tips to help you create wonderful jewellery from inexpensive materials.
(EBayer selling beads or jewellery components)

'Visit my About Me page for free weekly tips to help your eBay business grow quickly and prosper.
(eBayer selling packaging materials/ebooks/ wholesale products)

Incidentally, your tipsheet will indeed contain tips but its real purpose is to solicit orders for more of your products.

Once the visitor reaches your About Me page they find instructions as to how to contact you for the newsletter/tipsheet/updates, such as by phoning, emailing, visiting your web site.

Collect those email addresses, preferably using a specialist email newsletter and auto-responder service like aweber.com or manually if you're just starting out or on a tight budget. I use Aweber's system, which costs about £10 a month, and actually collects all email addresses for me from people giving contact details at my site or responding to a given email address. The system also allows me to create messages on auto-responder which can be timed or sent as a sequence of messages. It also allows people to unsubscribe without ever deleting names myself by hand.

Ideas for your newsletters and emails

- Send an email every week or so describing your new products on eBay, or otherwise available through affiliate deals, on your web site, etc.

This is how I made £100 while waiting for the kettle to boil.

I sell cufflinks on eBay and while looking for wholesale and dropship items I found a few companies offering big affiliate commissions on their cufflinks, one giving 10 per cent on high quality jewellery, watches and cufflinks.

I had just uploaded a site for marketing cufflinks outside of eBay and for starters I'd added that one affiliate company with my affiliate ID.

I'd already collected email addresses of more than 100 buyers of cufflinks on eBay, so I set the kettle to boil, opened my email account at aweber, clicked on 'Create New Mail', and keyed in one customer address as the main recipient and the rest went into the CC box. (Incidentally, the Outlook Express system on most computers works just as well but means you have to add and delete addresses manually).

My message was clear and simple, the heading was **SPECIAL OFFER CUFFLINKS AND SUPER DISCOUNTS JUST FOR YOU:** 'Thank you for buying from us on eBay. As a much valued customer I've arranged a very special deal for you with (the affiliate company) whose incredible Summer Sale starts today.

Go to www.blahblah.com and feast your eyes on a glorious array of fabulous quality cufflinks for yourself or the men in your life.

Don't forget to let me know if you find anything suitable and I'll give you £10 discount on any future purchase from my eBay shop at: .'

Now those other cufflinks weren't cheap, in fact the link on my site led to a ruby and diamond cufflink set costing well over £1,000. One of my customers bought a set that day. I expect my £100 plus to arrive very soon.

- **Send a newsletter each week of tips and ideas for people to benefit from your product and including short articles about the subject area.** Include mentions of other products to benefit them, either from your own stock or an affiliate company. This newsletter format is less threatening than an email openly asking recipients to visit some site potentially to buy. A newsletter is more discreet, seeming more like friendly advice and product recommendations than outright invitations to buy.

- **Legally, you must give people on your list a chance to unsubscribe. Do this by adding something like this at the end of the email or ezine/newsletter:** 'This newsletter is never sent unsolicited. You are receiving it because you requested it or because you are a customer of BLAH BLAH. However, if you no longer wish to receive our news updates and special offers simply send a blank email, subject UNSUBSCRIBE, to (your email address)'. Check regularly and delete names immediately on request; if you forget later it looks bad and could terminate your email account. Aim to move quickly to a professional email autoresponder service as soon as possible.

- Sending newsletters and emails is easy to do and very effective but you need an organised approach if you're to avoid a barrage of insults and spam accusations.

Footnote – why selling to past customers is more profitable than constantly targeting new buyers.

The 80/20 rule works in all areas of life and goes roughly like this:

Eighty per cent of profits come from twenty per cent of effort.

Twenty per cent of past buyers will become regular buyers.

Twenty per cent of product accounts for eighty per cent of takings.

The rule was invented by Pareto, hence 'Pareto's Theory' and, don't ask me why, but through experience I have found the 20/80 – 80/20 – rule actually does work to most areas of personal and business life.

As an example, years ago, when I began adding my buyers to database, I decided to highlight those who'd bought more than once. And yes, the figures were 1 in 5: twenty per cent were regular buyers. Every fifth customer gained became a regular buyer and, guess what, those one in five people accounted for eighty per cent of my profits from follow up mailings.

Don't just ask for money, demand it! Using a 'Call to Action' to generate orders NOW!

A call to action is a device used by top copywriters to create a sense of urgency for potential customers to request more information about a product or to buy right away.

Although most sellers shy from asking for money or an immediate order, it remains the best way to maximise profits in the shortest possible time.

Asking doesn't have to be rude, or intrusive, and can be accomplished with a single phrase in your listing or its title or sub-title, such as:

• Buy Now While the Discount Lasts.
• Buy Now While Stocks Last.
• Buy Today and Get Another One Free.
• Bid Now, Before Someone Beats You To It.
• Only Two Left – Buy Now While Stocks Last.

Buy Now and Get (XXXX) Free – Lasts This Week Only! (Try to make that freebie something people might buy in its own right but can't because it's only available as a freebie).

More ways to generate fast sales and impulse buys

• **Put your product on auction for ten days at the same price the product is available from your eBay shop**. Inside the listing, before you even mention the product say: 'Click HERE to visit my shop and buy at the same price right now without having to wait for the auction to end and without losing out to higher bidders'.

• **Sell BUY IT NOW but only for products you've tested and know their optimum price** (the price most commonly achieved at previous auction list-

ings for the item). Buy It Now is a great way to generate impulse buys and can be offered independently or alongside the auction option. When I had trouble selling my cufflinks at auction, starting price £9.99, I uploaded them BUY IT NOW for £9.99. They quickly sold and meant I could relist several times each week instead of waiting for seven day auctions to end.

• **A visitor who finds your product isn't quite what he wants right now might be interested in other items you already have or might source later.** How do you stop that person moving away and looking elsewhere to buy? Simple: add something like: 'If this isn't what you are looking for, email me with your requirements and I'll see if we have suitable items in stock. Contact me through my About Me page'. The About Me page incidentally, is the only place you are allowed to provide out of eBay contact details.

Use the 'Second Chance' feature to make repeat sales and more cash!

Unlike people selling one-off items, like rare antiques and collectors' items, most successful eBayers look for popular items with high markups, which can be quickly and easily replenished in bulk.

This example will illustrate why. Imagine you have a widget that costs you £10 a time and sells regularly at £20. Nice profits, and you can list the item any time you like in almost certain chance of a sale. (Some eBayers have thousands of repeat sale items and you'll soon understand why).

Back to your widget, and let's say ten people are bidding on one listing, all prepared to pay £15 upwards to own the item, which finally sells at £25. If this is an exclusive widget, that's your lot, you've made £15 (minus selling fees) and you can't ever list the product again.

Not so if you have several similar widgets available where you can make 'Second Chance Offers' –

the term is self-explanatory – to non-winning bidders, as many as you have products for whose bids generate a profit.

When an auction ends, assuming you had multiple bidders, all you do is log into your eBay account, click through to 'Selling' to the left of the screen, then 'Sold', find the appropriate listing and under the 'Action' column choose 'Second Chance Offer'. You'll be directed to another page showing non-winning bidders and their maximum bid amounts. Highlight those whose offer you accept and submit your Second Chance Offer.

Now wait, some will buy your widgets, a few might not, from experience I know most will. Personally, I've always thought it a bit unfair that the real winner pays more than 'losers', but there's a profit to be made, so go grab your share.

How to turn a simple compliments slip into a repeat backend income generator

I'm going to let you in on a secret now: this is the best income-generator I've ever discovered and it's already working wonders in my business.

Every time I fulfill an order, I print a page out of my computer, slice it in three, put one into my outgoing package, while the other two wait for sales of a similar product.

Actually, my precious secret's just a compliments slip, but one with a difference.

This slip doesn't just thank the recipient for buying, it also suggests other items that person might purchase, but those items aren't mine. I may not even know what these products look like, but I'll make money every time someone clicks and buys from the auction site printed on my slip.

Of course it seems you've heard it all before, but this time it's different.

For a start, every product has its own quite unique compliments slip; every buyer gets information about

sites they'll be very keen to visit; products will be closely related to what they've purchased already.

And I have hundreds of these compliments slips planned, all different, soon there'll be thousands, and each one will have its own unique domain name.

This isn't brain surgery. All I'm really doing is looking for companies offering affiliate commissions for products my customers might like to buy. I'm harnessing the power of back-end selling to almost guarantee close to one in five of my eBay buyers will visit the site mentioned on my compliments slip and buy through my affiliate link.

Each product or group of products has a different affiliate link, and a different web site. This is why:

You already know that raw affiliate links look much like this: www.avrilharper.com/cgi/?Merchant=ID123-908/Affiliate+ID=190984633&affiliatecom=50%&repeat=20blahblahblah

There isn't space for that on my compliments slip, and anyway no-one's going to key all that into their browser in the chance of finding something to interest them.

Most people build complex sites for their back-end sales, using professional designers, and making changes daily as new products arrive and others go out of stock. It's hard work, expensive, and totally unnecessary.

All you need is a simple page that transfers visitors to your supplying companies' sites through a simple message such as 'Click Here to Enter Site'. Using a technique called 'hyperlinking' you embed your affiliate details – that long line mentioned earlier – behind your chosen text. Such a site takes seconds to create, minutes to upload, and opens to reveal potentially thousands of products that earn you earn commission on every sale.

So that's it, in a nutshell, everyone who buys doggy stuff from my eBay listings gets a compliments slip highlighting my simple site linking to one of the UK's main providers of kennels, dog foods, dog toys, harnesses and leads, and much more besides.

Those who buy eBooks and business courses receive a compliments slip to my site linking to ClickBank's affiliate based products; buyers of paper collectibles are linked to big time sellers of price catalogues, collectors' books and newsletters.

It's small beer right now. I have just forty different compliments slips, but they'll grow by twenty or more each month. From now on I'll choose eBay products based on whatever affiliate opportunities can be found for back end sales.

Commissions vary between companies and there are lots of products and companies to choose from. It's a good idea to join an affiliate middleman company, like ClickBank or Affiliate Window, who operate on behalf of numerous sellers and rank companies according to popularity with the buying public and indicate potential earnings based on number of clicks from your own to suppliers' sites.

It's important to take your time choosing between products and supplying companies. As much time, effort and money goes into making several pounds per sale as earning a paltry fifty pence fixed fee per sale. Most companies give affiliates a fixed percentage of sale prices; others pay a token sum, invariably on the low side, whether visitors spend £20 or two thousand pounds. Optimise your earnings by seeking highest commissions on highest ticket products.

I'm still new to this technique but already I'm earning £20 and £30 every time someone buys eBooks from C B Mall's ClickBank portal via my page – http://www.smartfreelance.com

My site www.dog-breed.net links to hundred more products my dog-loving eBay customers might also find interesting. I've sold three kennels in the last week and numerous smaller items, all-in-all about £125 pure profit.

Here's what you need to copy my experience:

1) Products to sell on eBay which have back end selling potential. These can be the same or similar products to what people have purchased already on eBay, or they may compliment an eBay purchase.

2) An affiliate provider, either a supplying company or an affiliate network mediator offering lots of different products through numerous different companies, the likes of Affiliate Window (www.affiliatewindow.com), ClickBank (www.clickbank.com), and countless others.

3) Domain names and hosting space. Domain names should reflect product types such as www.dogstuff.com, www.papercollectibles.com, www.businessbooks.com. Incidentally, I dreamed those up in seconds, I haven't checked if they actually exist; if they do, they're not mine, they're just examples of good memorable domain names that are short and sweet and unlikely to trip-up even the world's worst typist. Domain names and hosting space are easily available with good deals available if you shop around. I recommend you have domain names and hosting space with one company, preferably a long-standing company with good credentials. For what it's worth, I use www.donhost.co.uk. They're excellent. And no, they're not paying me to say that.

4) Knowledge of how to create and upload a simple site with 'ENTER' hyperlinked to your affiliate url. Very easy, yet it took me months to learn this quite simple, straightforward task. But then I had no one showing me how to do it. You do have help, in the form of a short report highlighting the basics for you to download at: www.1st-in-auctions.com/uploading.html

That's it, a great idea, one you can copy right away. And, best of all, this is the subject of a special report I'm writing now for our readers which my publishers will tell you all about in a coming email. It won't be expensive and we'll also be offering hosting space to our readers as an optional part of the package.

Cashing in on seasons, anniversaries and special events

How to make more money in six weeks than some people make all year!

Christmas is almost here and it's absolutely, positively, without doubt, the most exciting time for new and veteran eBayers!

You may not have sold on eBay last festive season, but I did, and let me tell you it was so wonderfully profitable. Almost everything I listed sold, many items attracted multiple bids generating lots of second chance offers. I made more money last December than I made during the whole of the summer months. Even better, I kept careful records of seasonal best sellers, order-pulling marketing tactics, in the UK and other eBay country sites, which I'll tell you all about here and at our members web site.

Research company, Interactive Media in Retail Group (IMRG), says that half the UK population shops online at Christmas. In fact, sales in the six weeks run-up to Christmas account for more than fifty per cent of many retailers' annual takings. That was certainly my experience on eBay last year purely because I planned my selling campaign several months ahead of the big event. In fact, sales in the six weeks run-up to Christmas account for more than fifty per cent of many retailers' annual takings. It's a time when people really get to grips with spending, and time for our readers to plan their selling campaigns several months ahead of the big event.

Benefits of selling anniversary, seasonal and special event products

• **High Niche Market Potential.** At Christmas, almost everyone thinks Christmas, and much the same goes for Valentine's Day, Easter, Halloween. The result is niche markets that last just a few weeks, sometimes just days, but they're potentially

most profitable of all. Much the same goes for anniversaries such as a historical event (this year marks the 400 anniversary of the Gun Powder Plot and it's one hundred years since Las Vegas was founded), big time sports events, such as the Olympics and Football World Cup.

• **History Repeats Itself.** Seasons and anniversaries come and go, and what you learn one year will benefit coming years' endeavors. You'll learn which listings to repeat and which to bin, which manufacturers to buy from, while all the time building a list of enquirers and buyers for future promotions.

• **Great Research Potential.** Every season, anniversary and special event comes with ready made ideas for you to copy next time round. Be careful, however, and learn to distinguish between legal and illegal copying of other people's ideas, products and intellectual copyrights. When you know the distinction, record most successful and spectacular eBay listings, buy as many advertising publications as possible for your target audience, visit web sites, save marketing emails, compile a huge swipe file of print and online marketing ideas and initiatives. Especially product ideas!

• **Sense of Urgency To Buy. Most seasons**, anniversaries, special events, are of limited duration and people know if they don't buy soon, the ads. will quickly disappear. There's a sense of urgency attached which forces people to buy NOW, unlike non-time-sensitive promotions which might be put to one side to study later, and promptly forgotten!

Big Christmas stock acquisition tip

I got carried away this morning, looking for all-year Christmas selling sites for our readers, and finding much more.

It wasn't just sites, I also found plenty of product and marketing ideas.

For Christmas sites, I keyed 'Christmas + site' into www.google.com and found hundreds to choose from. As usual the best right on top of the pile, with some brilliant idea-generators listed later. Next time I have a few hours spare I'll continue my search.

For now, these are the sites I particularly liked, which include lots of great product ideas For you to emulate or even buy to resell:

www.thechristmasshop.co.uk – there's a physical shop on London Bridge.

www.christmastimeuk.com – physical shop in Fillingham, near Lincoln.

www.nutcrackerchristmasshop.co.uk – physical bases in Edinburgh, Crieff and Stratford upon Avon.

Outside the UK I found:

www.islandchristmasshop.com – United States.
www.christmasshop.dk – Denmark..
www.outbackboutique.com – United States.

Tips

If you find a product you'd like to sell which looks cheap enough to make a significant profit, do more checks. These tips apply to most product types, not just seasonal items.

• **Americans love Christmas tree ornaments and you might safely buy quality items in the UK to relist on eBay.com.** Generally, the more upmarket the product, the more Americans will like your Christmas ornaments, especially hand-made, glass blown, hand decorated one-off specimens. You'll find some wonderful ideas at those sites listed earlier.

• **Does cheap mean poor quality?** If you're importing the product, is it safe, legal, will it pass UK safety inspections? Poor quality toys and non-shatterproof decorations with sharp pieces may be banned from entering the UK or could get you fined for negligence if injury later results. Contact local Customs and Excise departments about rules regarding import of toys and other potentially harmful products. For more information visit http: www.hmrc.gov.uk

• **Some products are banned from entering the postal services such as fireworks and some Christmas crackers and batteries**, and anything potentially flammable or explosive. See: www.royalmail.com for details.

• **Is the product Vatable?** If so, is VAT extra? Or is VAT included and can you claim it back? Remember you may also have to charge VAT on these products, except where you sell exclusively outside the EC.

• **Are import duties or other taxes payable on products imported to the UK?** Check first before ordering and don't buy until you know all costs of buying and fulfilling products and find profit margins acceptable.

• **How much is delivery to your business or direct to your customers?** Is packing included in the price? If packing is extra, how much is it; is it realistic or a sneaky way to bump up prices?

• **Is the product cheaper elsewhere?** The lowest prices invariably come when you buy direct from the maker. A little research pays handsome dividends. To illustrate, this morning I found some wonderful Christmas novelties on sale in Edinburgh. Priced £2 each I was sure they'd fetch £10 plus in the USA. Still seeking Christmas novelties online, I found the same items selling in London at less than half the Scottish prices and discovered this second supplier was also manufacturer for the product.

• **When you find a product you'd like to sell, search for the product by Name to find the same item at lower prices as well as other items that might prove more suitable.** For example, having found a Christmas tree decoration depicting a London Policeman, I keyed in the description of the product into www.google.com like this: 'London + policeman + Christmas + tree + decoration'. I chose Google's 'image' option which returns pictures rather than just words and found lots of policemen-shaped baubles to choose from, including the exact same model I'd seen earlier and at much lower cost. Those + signs in a search box will return sites containing all of your keywords as opposed to countless more sites returning one or two of your chosen words. For example 'London policeman Christmas tree decoration' without the + signs, will return all manner of sites, a few containing information for eBay resellers alongside many others having little or no relation to seasonal goods. Use the + signs and you won't waste time learning which Bobby dressed the Christmas tree in some London Nick last year!

• **Look for sites offering trade facilities or with their own affiliate programme.** These are firms most likely to allow others use of their graphics and sales materials and you already stand to profit from basic trade or affiliate discounts even where you match the supplying company's retail price.

• **Where possible visit physical stores before buying. Most have additional products to those shown online**. So you'll probably find items exclusive to your eBay listings and you'll get to test and inspect items before buying.

• **Find high quality, low cost Christmas decorations and novelty goods at local church fairs and craftwork shows.** You'll find these advertised in local newspapers, usually at the weekend, more so during November and December. Some wonderful products are available from skilled craftworkers charging low prices to increase church funds and having no business experience or inclination to market products by other means. So don't be mean, don't haggle, pay the asking price and, if you find a real bargain, offer a donation and get makers' contact details for future buys.

eBay Selling Tips

• **Mention 'Christmas' in your title**. It's amazing how few people have no idea what they want to buy as gifts for family and friends, so they'll choose just by keying 'Christmas' into eBay's search engine and buy from whatever turns up.

• **Offer a fast delivery service.** Join eBay's 'Get It Fast' programme for a special mention of fast delivery on your listing: http://pages.ebay.co.uk/help/buy/gif.html

• **Have the gift icon show on your listings**. Learn how at: http://pages.ebay.co.uk/help/buy/browsing_gifticons.html

At that page you'll also learn how to attract more bids by offering:

Gift Wrap/Gift Card
Express Shipping
Ship to Gift Recipient

Keeping up-to-date with anniversaries, seasons, special events

We all know when Christmas occurs, and Valentine's Day, too. But do you know when 'Teacher's Day' is, or 'Firefighters' Day', 'Hotdog Day'? No, neither did I, but I do now, as you will also if you go to your favourite search engine, I like Google, and key in:

'Firefighters Day' or similar option. You'll get lots of results some including additional holidays and special days for your product finding expeditions.

Another great place to look is: http://www.infoplease.com/ipa/A0875655.html

More ways to locate special days to focus upon:

• **Key '100 anniversary' into your favourite search engine.** Today on Google I learned that 2005 marks Rolls Royce and Ford Motors 100th anniversary (I wonder if they are celebrating); it's 100 years since Winterville in Georgia, USA was founded, and more.

• **I keyed the same combination into eBay.com and discovered items already being sold to commemorate such as Harley Davidson's 100 anniversary,** the Disney Corporation's 100 years of existence, and much more.

• **Look for sites promoting special events. I keyed 'Guy Fawkes 400'** into Google and found this fabulous site, selling fireworks, but also listing anniversaries and special events when fireworks might be required. Note that fire works are banned from sale on eBay and can not be sent through the post, so use this as an example, not a recommendation. Visit:

http://www.fireworksarcade.co.uk/Guy-Fawkes-400-Year-Anniversary.htm

• **Visit www.shop.com** for lots of information about anniversaries and some great products to integrate into your business.

• **Visit:**

http://news.bbc.co.uk/onthisday/default.stm for information about anniversary events but notice these are today's events, it's too late to capitalise on them right now, but, who knows, if you're around in 25 years time these are the events you could be making big money from.

• **Other places to source information:**
http:www.thisdayin music.com

Writers' and Artist's Yearbook by A and C Black includes a diary of events for writers and other artists but it's just as useful for eBay sellers, too.

Hot selling products that cost little or nothing

Just because it's free or doesn't cost much, doesn't mean your product won't bring high profits on eBay. Let the 'One Man's Meat is Another Man's Poison' theory work in reverse for you and help you find items other people sell at a pittance, or even give free of charge, guide you to acquiring some of the most profitable items on eBay.

Every day our researchers search for ideas for this regular feature in *eBay Confidential*. With several years experience even we are shocked at the amazing mark-ups possible from items we thought worthless or too plentiful to justify easy profits.

Postcards: How to buy a card for 10p and sell it for £50 or more!

Postcards are one of the most popular and profitable products selling on eBay and an option open to everyone, even without specialist experience – subject to following a few simple rules you'll learn about here.

I've been selling postcards on and off for about thirty years, with reasonable success, until I found eBay when things suddenly got a whole lot better.

Prior to finding eBay I sold cards at collectors' fairs, being local events where sales were limited, and profits nothing flash. Customers at collectors' fairs wanted largely local cards, views of nearby towns and cities, with one or two specialist collectors of subject cards but never enough to make it worthwhile stocking cards for them.

So I and dozens of regular postcard dealers at collectors' fairs stocked 'views' better known as 'topographical' cards from within a hundred miles or so radius from our own homes. And no matter how many wonderful non-local cards one encountered at auction, no matter how low the prices, they just weren't worth buying. Those you did buy hogged storage space and eventually got damaged and torn. Hardly anyone wanted them locally.

Today it's so very different, thanks to eBay, where I stay home and reach customers thousands of miles away, in Australia, America, South Africa, keen to buy and pay high prices for postcards I pick up for pennies from flea market and collectors' fair sellers still oblivious to eBay. Let's hope they stay that way!

Follow these tips to find postcards for pennies with potential to generate high profits:

- **The best selling postcards are generally pre-1939**, or slightly later for unusual or limited production items.

- **Do not pay high prices for anything, single card or album**, until you understand what makes one postcard worth hundreds of pounds and another practically nothing.

- **Note that early view cards of churches, castles, cathedrals, beach scenes, and such are almost worthless**, unless some other factor such as postmark, special event, publisher, etc., increases the value. That said, nothing is certain on eBay where on more than one occasion I've made £50, sometimes more, on cards I thought expensive at ten pence each.

- **Generally speaking, views that could have been created any day** over several decades, such as park scenes, churches, where nothing much changes, fetch the lowest prices. Rare events, such as Royal Visits, road accidents, Suffragette marches and such, even on the stalest view, can fetch hundreds of pounds apiece.

- **Valuable collectors' postcards include** real photographic street scenes (preferably with trams, people, horses and carts), social history (Suffragettes, Jarrow Marchers), disasters (Titanic, Mining and Railway accidents), special events (staff outside newly opened shop, executions), royalty (especially Russian), artist-drawn glamour cards (Raphael Kirchner, Alphonse Mucha, Fabiano), motoring and railways, art nouveau, fantasy cards, hold-to-light, and others you'll read about in *'Picture Postcard Values'* published annually by P and D Smith and available from various sources including Reflections of a Bygone Age (www.postcardcollecting.org.uk) who also publish *'Picture Postcard Monthly'*.

- **Generally speaking, the older the card, the more valuable it might be**, although some modern cards are valuable for other reasons, because they are autographed, for example, or belonged to a famous owner. Cards personally signed by John Lennon, for example, or Laurel and Hardy, fetch a huge premium over and above their plain portrait counterparts.

- **Look for items available in bulk at auction**, from flea markets and collectors' fairs. Price is generally low as most collectors lack money and inclination to buy in bulk. If you can't tell a rare card from a common one, aim to pay 10p each across the board and list cards with starting price 99p. Market forces will distinguish cards worth just 99p or less from others worth many times more. You might lose money once or twice, some cards will remain unsold, others might sell below their real market value, but based on our experience, eight out of ten cards will reach more than starting price, and you will still make money.

- **Your best chance of buying high value cards at a pittance** is in small country auction houses with poorly advertised promotions meaning few specialist dealers or collectors on the day. Rain, snow, heavy winds also keep turnout low.

- **Look for mixed or specialist bundles of postcards**, say 101 North East England, 2,000 dogs/cats, 24 railways, etc. In this case, few general dealers or collectors want all cards in the batch so bidding can be low. Remember the 10p across the board rule but only if cards are in reasonably decent, untorn, unblemished condition. See the next tip.

- **Expect exceptions to every rule**. A really tatty photographic postcard of an un-named football team fetched £100 plus on eBay recently due to the diligence of one or two collectors who recognised the team as Manchester United in the early 1900s.

- **Avoid ex-dealers' stocks unless better items are included and the price is low**. Recognise them from prices pencilled on the reverse; lots of different recipients (most original collections bear maximum two or three different recipients and addresses); huge selection with no real gems (all genuine vintage and modern collections contain some better items).

- **Countless copies of one design or subject indicate low value, even worthless cards**. Examples: deckle-edged greetings cards depicting flowers, fruit (most people experience birthdays, Christmas,

Easter, New Year; fruit/flowers are common subjects); printed views of churches, cathedrals, bridges (view could be recreated any day of the week, printing always long run); photos of people (unless famous/infamous); unknown beauties (exception: nude studies, bordering on risque, by famous artists, notably Kirchner, Mucha).

- **Specialise in one or two main areas,** say animals, military, stars of stage and screen. You'll generate repeat buyers and a great mailing list for off-eBay promotions. You'll also find traders in other items offering their unwanted cards to you in bulk as opposed to having to list items individually themselves. *Silly people!*

   Bear in mind a card even the experts consider worth little or nothing can fetch a great price at auction with two serious bidders and money to spend. The 'I wanna have it' principle reigns supreme on eBay and accounts for many shock results. Like my ping pong cards, and carp cufflinks, worn and torn views of many different places, and...

Charity shops

It pays eBayers to visit shops run by the likes of Oxfam and the British Heart Foundation, where nearly new items can be purchased at a fraction of their true market value.

   Veteran bargain-hunters and eBayers ourselves, we've picked up everything from floor-coverings to dog baskets, even a hamster cage and complete set of encyclopaedias in our local high street charity shops.

   These shops are also the perfect place to find quality clothing which might need just a wash and iron to sell on eBay, or maybe you could add a few new features to make good money. Belts, new buttons, embroidered pockets, all make a big difference to garments and profits.

   For work and leisure clothing, charity shops are great places to buy nearly-new at really low prices and, as any regular charity shopper will know, it isn't unusual for prices to be cut to the bone to make space for new stock arriving almost daily.

Tips

- Regular visits are vital to take advantage of fantastic reductions on already heavily discounted items.

- Ask your local shop when their new stock goes on display and beat others to new items and last minute bargains on outgoing stock.

- There's more to charity shops than quality clothing, and you can expect to find vast reductions on giftware, toys, books, magazines, and so much more.

- For an idea of savings on high resale value items this is what we found in our local Oxfam shop just a short while ago:

- A designer wedding dress for £50 (original price £1,000).

- A large children's playhouse selling in the high street for over £100 being offered for just £15.

- A take-your-pick rail of M & S ladies' dresses at £2.50 each.

- An album of vintage postcards – wait for it, priced at £20 – which from our extensive interest in buying and selling such items we know is worth at least £300. Actually much, much more, but we don't like to brag.

- Quality greetings cards – new – looking better and costing less than anything you'll find in specialist card shops.

- Rows and rows of paperback books at 10p each.

Further information

- Key 'List of Charity Charity Shops UK' into www.google.com, tick the box for UK pages only, and feast your eyes on countless charity shops all over the UK.

- Check out The Association of Charity Shops http://www.charityshops.org.uk/members.html lists hundreds of UK charity shop members of their organisation.

The public domain

Typically 'Public Domain' describes literary, musical, artistic works, which are no longer protected by copyright and others that were never subject to copyright. Laws vary by country, but are easy to follow.

It's amazing how many people shun or just overlook this hugely profitable area. Some I've spoken to fear being sued for breach of copyright, others think no one is interested in work created so long ago, yet more people know about the public domain but they don't understand how it works.

From your letters we know many of our subscribers are interested in finding and promoting out of copyright books and pictures, to a lesser extent musical and other artistic works. So much so, we'll make this a regular feature of our newsletter. We'll cover items already in the public domain and others about to shed copyright and open profitable opportunities for our readers.

Currently all items published in the USA before 1923 are in the public domain, meaning you can virtually copy them at will. At the risk of sounding unpatriotic, I pick entirely from US titles, where copyright laws are clear cut and easier to understand. Just my opinion.

In the UK copyright typically extends to 70 years from the end of the calendar year in which the creator died (not the same as 70 years since the creator's death), with some other restrictions as explained concisely in *Writers' and Artists' Yearbook* available from all main reference libraries. The book also covers US and other world copyright issues.

Worked example: artist reprints

The UK's seventy year rule is great news for anyone keen to offer reprinted works of artist Cecil Aldin who passed on, conveniently for our purposes, in 1935, seventy years ago. He died on 6th January 1935 as my visit to www.google.com showed on the first page of search results for 'Cecil Aldin died'. So the 70 year rule starts at the end of 1935, not on 6th January, 1935, and ends in the final seconds of 2005. His works are hugely popular on eBay, I know because I sell them, but until now I've sold prints taken from books and magazines containing Aldin's stunning dog and animal prints. Come January 1st,

2006, I'll be selling reprints, items created by scanning an original book plate or print into my computer, arranging it neatly on an A4 template, reproducing it on quality art paper.

I sell books too, on paper and CD, taken mainly from works in the public domain. Notice I said 'Mainly' because there are several ways to profit from other writers' work with no fees or royalties of any kind to pay.

How to create a book in day and profit from it for life

Though not strictly public domain, there are millions of articles, ebooks, reports and other texts which you can publish and sell. Best of all, these books are unique, yours alone, not available from any other source.

It can be done using books known to be in the public domain or by combining articles and other writings carrying resell rights or termed 'copyright free'.

- **Items in the public domain.** Choose anything published in the USA before 1923. Publish 'as is' or edit the work, add your own ideas, updated old-fashioned language, create a new title. Sell it on paper, as a download, on CD. Find suitable works via search engines or eBay or visit sites specialising in works in the public domain. For books the best is Project Gutenberg: www.gutenberg.com; for music try: www.pdinfo.com; for artists visit: www.artoftheprint.com

- **Copyright Free (and similar) works**. Hundreds of authors provide articles and longer works free of charge for others to publish with the author's contact details. It's a way of getting others to promote the author's business via links included in the article. So a vet specialising in homeopathic remedies might write articles about healing herbs with a mention of how to contact him for treatment or supplies. Another might specialise in web site marketing, or collecting teddy bears, potty training, virtually any subject. You benefit by selecting articles, from the same or different writers, usually on a common subject, which are combined into one text of a similar font. Each article becomes a chapter in your book, with the author's mention – called a 'resource box' – printed last. Create a list of chapters, basically authors' titles for individual articles.

Paginate your text, meaning each chapter begins on a new page, use bigger bolder fonts for titles, include the author's name and specialty. Create a title for your book, add your name as editor, add your copyright notice. There's the first book out of the way, now do another. One caution, a minority of writers set conditions, such as only publishing on web sites, not selling through auction, and so on. They are few and very far between but it's best to check first by reading conditions or contacting authors direct. I always contact authors direct, tell them about my plan, ask if they approve? I've never been refused.

Where to find articles

Find articles yourself via search engines like Google and Yahoo. Key such as 'articles free' or 'articles training dogs', and similar.

Alternatively visit the following popular article sites:

http://www.powerhomebiz.com
http://1st-in-articles.com
http://www.articlecentral.com
http://www.articlecity.com
http://www.ideamarketers.com
http://www.goarticles.com
http://www.certificate.net

There are many more some of which we have listed for you at: www.1st-in-articles.com/Articles.html

Be careful

Like many of our readers, I'm fascinated by the public domain and the sheer volume of opportunities waiting for sellers on eBay. I've profited from numerous ideas myself, and discovered many rules and misconceptions to safeguard myself, and our readers, from making costly mistakes.

This is what I've learned and please be aware, rules change; what applies today might be outdated tomorrow. Keep on visiting the Public Domain section of our subscribers only website for updates – www.1st-in-auctions.com

Tips

• **The public domain is not to be confused with reproduction or manufacturing rights.**

Reproduction and manufacturing rights, where, for example, someone gives you a master copy of their book or product with rights to reproduce that item does not put it in the public domain. Public domain is largely based on time passed since a work was created and typically means that copyright has expired or perhaps never existed at all. Reproduction and manufacturing rights are a concession, usually passed by the product owner, allowing others to reproduce his work, but rarely does copyright also pass to the recipient. Public domain rights last indefinitely; reproduction rights can be time limited or otherwise withdrawn or restricted.

• **Public domain items can typically be amended**, changed, reshaped at will, and copyright belongs to no one. Not so reproduction and marketing rights where the original creator retains copyright and rarely allows others to alter his product. There are exceptions, as where authors allow others to use their work, even make changes, add their own name as author, and so on. Be careful: resell rights titles are wonderful sellers on eBay, but mistakes can be costly and can even get you expelled from eBay. Always ask before assuming what rights you have in a product.

• **Just because you own the original work, such as a painting or original final draft of a book or piece of music**, does not necessarily mean you also own copyright in the item. Nor does it mean you can make and sell copies of your original product. Recently, on television, an artist explained that he had sold an original painting from which he earned large sums from limited edition signed prints. Asked why he sold the painting and, by implication the reprint rights, he insisted he had only sold the painting, not his intellectual copyright in the item. Someone else has the painting, he has the copyright and subsequent marketing rights. His claims were verified by the programme's legal team.

Specific product categories

Jewellery

Jewellery is one of the best selling products on eBay and, unlike most other popular categories, the astute seller can face little or no competition for his products, while still reaching millions of potential buyers and achieving unusually high profit margins.

Sounds perfect, a dream come true, which with experience we know to be true.

Follow my advice, based on experience not just research, become that astute seller.

Unusually, well I thought so, eBay's jewellery market looks to be dominated by men and family set ups, and accounts for the majority of top UK PowerSellers. So gentlemen, don't be deterred, this isn't women's work at all. I spoke to several PowerSellers for this feature, two men, one woman, and asked for one tip to benefit our readers they gave the same reply:

Focus, specialise, don't just sell jewellery, sell a specific type of jewellery.

Choosing a Category

eBay UK has eleven main categories for 'Jewellery and Watches', each with several sub-categories, which divide again into tiny niche markets which are the most profitable of all to focus upon.

Those main categories are:

Beads
Costume Jewellery
Ethnic and Tribal Jewellery
Findings/Jewellery Making
Fine Jewellery
Jewellery Boxes
Loose Gemstones
Men's Jewellery
Vintage and Antique Jewellery
Watches
Other Jewellery

Taking one at random, I chose 'Costume Jewellery', the category further breaks down into:

Anklets/Ankle Chains
Bangles
Body Jewellery
Bracelets
Brooches/Pins
Charms/Charm Bracelets
Chokers
Earrings
Hair/Head Jewellery
Necklaces/Chains
Pendants/Lockets
Rings
Sets
Mixed Lots
Other Costume Jewellery

Go into any of those sub-categories and you'll find further breakdowns and ultimately very tight niche markets that are easy to target and potentially the most profitable of all for you to focus upon.

Where do you start, what are your choices?

- **Sell anything and everything within the overall category 'Jewellery'**. Not always a good idea, as our PowerSeller experts suggested, unless you're an expert already. Otherwise you'll spend most of your time researching, describing and valuing your finds. You need to focus more closely, look for a niche, choose one or two items to learn about quickly, create descriptions to suit similar products, work from templates that need just a few changes to suit every item you list.

- **Specialise in one type of jewellery or maker or a specific theme, such as belt buckles**, Native American creations, specific designers like Pilgrim, particular themes such as Masonic Tie Pins. Learning time is much shorter now as you move closer to a niche market, with restricted competition, but still time-consuming and potentially risky.

- **Specialise in all types of jewellery of a specific quality**, such as: vintage, all gold, second hand. Copious time spent studying and listing individual items here is compensated for by less competition in these areas. Vintage items by their nature are limited, gold is expensive, second hand items are rarely available in bulk. The majority of eBay sellers like new items, available in bulk, inexpensively, with little work involved. That rarely happens in this category.

- **Craftsman and hand-made or hand-finished jewellery**. My particular favourite and your best chance of listing one-off items for a huge target audience.

Exclusive jewellery is hugely popular on eBay where just a few suppliers dominate the scene. Find yourself a designer or make stock yourself and you can literally produce items on demand, without ever paying up front or holding stock, and facing little or no competition. Read what was said earlier about locating jewellery designers and makers at craft and trade shows and find someone willing to let you sell their goods exclusively.

Study eBay's top jewellery sellers

Go to http://pulse.ebay.co.uk, click on 'Jewellery and Watches' in the search box at the left of the screen, on the next page find some of the UK's main suppliers. Study them a while, look at what they are selling, how many items they list each day.

Very quickly you'll notice several things they all have in common.

- **Regular best selling items.** Check their completed auctions, see how many items they've sold, at what prices, study bidder numbers and how many second chance offers were possible. You will be amazed.

- **Few if any listings end without bids**. Many have 20 bidders or more, huge second chance potential, and early indication of a regular best selling product to list week after week.

- **Low listing fees**. Knowing most items will achieve high prices, there's little to lose and lots to gain by avoiding reserve amounts and using low starting prices, commonly 99p. Ninety-Nine pence represents 15p for the listing, same again for the gallery picture. List one hundred items and you pay just £15.00!!

- **Fewer listings required to generate good profits**. Unlike counterparts listing hundreds of pieces of widely differing jewellery, *hoping* some will sell, these eBayers list a few select items, ten to thirty is common, which they *know* will sell, fetch high prices, and multiple sales.

- **Less time listing,** means more time to spend finding new products, checking test results, making second chance offers.

Ideas

- **Increase the perceived value of your items.** Most stock from wholesalers, designers, makers, comes wrapped in tissue paper, rarely boxed. Add a presentation box and increase your profits significantly. For example, my youngest daughter sells lapel pins, costing her 50 pence each. They sell like hot cakes at £4.99 each, without a box. With a presentation box, price 40p, sometimes less, they're easy sellers at ten pounds plus.

- **Buy your boxes on eBay where many dealers specialise.** They cost as little as 10p each but they vary in quality and can actually make your item look cheaper boxed than otherwise. Choose quality, leather or leather-look boxes with covered tops not plastic which looks cheap and tatty. Avoid boxes bearing another company's name as are often sold on eBay. You could break Trade Description laws putting your jewellery into their boxes and you are missing the chance to brand your own products. Find presentation boxes by searching on eBay for 'jewellery display box', or similar.

- **Brand your jewellery by adding a tiny slip inside the box**, giving your company name, web site url, eBay shop, and such. It's a great way to generate later sales to public and resellers. See the next tip for an idea you can copy.

- **Include a discount coupon with your product**, offering reductions on future sales to those who've purchased already. Try this: open a text file on your computer, *Miscrosoft Word* is good, use portrait format, section the page into three equal horizontal section. Type the same message in one and cut and paste into the others, making three compliments slips to accompany your products. Say something like:

With Compliments

Jewellery With Passion

jewellery@myaddress.com

eBay shop: http: xxxxxxxxxxxxxxxxxxxxxxxxxxxxx

Thank you for buying one of our products. We aim to please so kindly leave feedback to let us know your package has arrived safely, and we'll reciprocate within 48 hours. As a thank you for your custom this slip entitles you to £x off any item in our eBay shop **Jewellery With Passion** (substitute your shop name), purchased on or before (date in here, use a separate rubber date stamp rather than typing it on computer, it looks more urgent and personal).

Best wishes
Ima Nee-Bayer

Where to obtain stock

Suppliers are plentiful and it's wise to search for firms willing to let you sell their goods exclusively on eBay.

• **Dropship and Wholesale Suppliers sites**

• **Specialist jewellery and non-specialist wholesalers** such as those listed later and others you'll find advertising in stock magazines like *Trader* and *Exchange and Mart* or exhibiting at Trade Shows which you'll usually find listed in *Trader* and specialist trade journals. Visit your local business library where you'll find most national and international trade journals. Get the address of your local Business Library (not the same as Public or Reference Library) from 'Business Enterprise' groups in *Yellow Pages*.

• **Jewellery Designers and Makers** you'll also find listed in publications and directories located in main Business Libraries, see the previous tip. Another great way to find them is via search engines – key in 'jewellery designer Durham' or variations to suit your requirements.

• **Local craft fairs and craft markets**. Find them advertised in local newspapers, usually on Friday night or Saturday morning, under 'Fairs', 'Days Out', or similar. Visit a few, gather business cards from exhibitors making jewellery, buy a few items to test the market on eBay.

• **Local auctions**. These are great places to buy second hand jewellery and sometimes complete job lots from retired and liquidated jewellers. Find them advertising in local newspapers, usually at the weekend. Most regional newspapers have a special Auctions section. If you're uncertain, study *Willing's Press Guide* in local reference libraries where you'll find all local, regional and national newspapers listed with address and phone numbers. Contact a few, ask about special auction sections, request a free sample copy or order from your newsagent.

• **Other**, including jewellery shops, pawnbrokers, sellers' advertisements in local newspapers, agents and wholesalers (some specialise in one-off or limited edition hand crafted items), import bulletins, and more as we'll discuss in future issues of *eBay Confidential*.

Sporting goods

One of the largest eBay UK categories, 'Sporting Goods' currently comprises 168816 items, about three-quarters actively selling, many with multiple bids.

That's a massive marketplace, and the nearest I've seen to niche marketing heaven.

With about 40 plus different categories, one for all major sports, most with double figure sub-categories, in less than an hour I'd found plentiful areas attracting heavy bidding and featuring surprisingly few specialist dealers. These markets are wide open for anyone to target and dominate right now.

Some areas are highly competitive, such as football shirts and exercise equipment. Not surprising when a football shirt sells every five minutes on eBay and a myriad of high profit fitness and exercise listings is attracting double figure bids and lots of prospective new owners.

Competition might be high but, as you'll soon discover, rapid turnover and multiple second chance offer potential is exactly what makes these areas well

---

worth considering for your business.

It's one of the fastest growing markets

• **Television brought sports to the masses**, never more so than today with countless televised sports programmes and specialist sports channels. But people are no longer mere spectators, many are participants too and in need of special clothing, accessories, tools and equipment.

• **In our increasingly health conscious society people use sports and exercise to keep fit and to enjoy themselves**. But we're time conscious too and a high percentage of people are opting for home gyms and exercise bikes in preference to exercising or cycling away from home. These are amongst the very best sellers across the whole of eBay UK and responsible for creating more high level PowerSellers than virtually any other product category.

• **Buyers of sporting goods are among the most fashion conscious of buyers** and will regularly discard perfectly good clothing and equipment in favour of the latest design.

• **People are living longer and enjoying healthier lives**, meaning more time to exercise and participate in sports. All makes for a thriving market, growing bigger by the day.

• **There are definite seasons and patterns in sports:** football in autumn and winter, tennis in summer, new marathons to run, new golf courses springing up alongside sprawling housing and industrial complexes. Every new season, every sports fad, every time Britain wins a major sports championship, we see sales of sporting goods reach record highs.

More reasons to focus on sporting goods

• **Most buyers are passionate about their chosen sport**, they love buying new clothing and equipment, and they're willing to spend big time to have the best especially in high status sports. For 'high status' sports read: golf, cricket, equestrian, skiing, and more besides. You really could list just a handful of repeat items for these sports and make regular

high profits all year round.

• **The Sporting Goods category is home to some of the highest priced items attracting multiple bidding on eBay**, yet overheads are low by comparison to others listing hundreds of different items for low unit profits. So if you list a canoe on eBay, starting price £999, profit £200 plus, and you sell to winner and multiple second chance buyers, profits say £1,000, you'll pay just £2 for a basic listing and a little more for pictures and optional extra selling features. Compare that to someone listing ten different items in a highly competitive field, like books and CDs, hoping to sell at £4.99 each. They'll pay £3.50 for listing and gallery picture, typically achieve few or no second chance sales and raise a maximum forty nine pounds ninety pence, minus overheads. There's no doubt about it, those high ticket, high demand, high repeat sales products dotted all over the Sporting Goods category are the ones to go for. Best of all, I researched this area for you and soon I'll reveal my chosen best sellers for you to copy.

• **So popular are some sporting goods you'll find sellers specialising in just one item**, sometimes a solitary design, like the following eBayers: Bumblewoof sells around 85 high price trampolines each month at almost £200 a time; warehouse-robot sells mainly dirt bikes and averages almost 1000 sales a month. I found many more one item sellers using the following technique.

Do it yourself guide to sourcing high ticket one product sellers *

* And a few more marketing a handful of prolific high profit products.

Go to eBay.co.uk, scroll down and, on the left, from the long list of categories, click on 'Sporting Goods'. Next page, choose any main category, like 'Football' or 'Paintballing', click on a sub-category, any will do. This is digging deep in a niche, focussing on comparatively few listings within the overall sub-category, and chances are repeat listings will show several to a page. Check the seller by clicking through one or two multiple featured listings, look for feedback score of one thousand plus, preferably several thousand. We're looking for big time sellers, not one hit wonders. Click to view sellers' other items. Make a note of prolific one product sellers and pay regular visits to check sales remain consistent before seeking similar products for your business.

Find several sellers focusing on one same-kind or similar item and you're onto a winner. They're not listing for fun, these items are major best sellers, the market's a long way from saturated. These are the kind of products to source for your business. But be careful, the next tip tells why.

BIG TIP

When you find these high demand, big ticket items, don't get complacement, there's always someone looking to steal your best ideas. So look for additional items to sell, either more one-off products or other items to market alongside most prolific sellers. Buyers of swimming pools need cleaning equipment, for example, outdoor trampolines need covers as protection from snow and rain. In my case people buying dog kennels also need dog beds and leads, toys and training equipment, and much more besides. Visit my 'boxersforever' account to see what I mean.

Find your niche in one of these eBay UK sporting goods categories

American Football... Archery... Badminton... Baseball... Basketball... Bowling (Ten-Pin)... Bowls... Boxing... Camping... Canoeing and Kayaking... Climbing/Mountaineering... Cricket... Cycling... Darts... Equestrian... Exercise and Fitness... Fishing... Football... Football Shirts... Golf... Gymnastics... Hiking... Hockey... Hunting... Inline and Roller Skating... Kitesurfing... Martial Arts... Paintballing... Rugby... Running and Athletics... Sailing... Scooters... Scuba and Snorkelling... Skateboarding... Skiing... Snowboarding... Snooker and Pool... Squash... Surfing... Swimming... Table Tennis... Tennis... Waterskiing and... Wakeboarding... Windsurfing... Other Sporting Goods.

Sticking my neck out – big ticket items I would sell in the sporting goods category

Were I working full-time on eBay I would look for maybe one hundred different big ticket items, with high profit margins and plenty of eager buyers.

I'd expect to list those 100 items at least once a week, possibly daily if I chose Buy It Now and sales were good. I'd budget on £3 per listing, so £300 minimum per week.

Let's say I made just £20 per item unit profit, so a trampoline costing me, say £100, goes for £120 with two second chance offers. That's £60 profit per listing, it could be more, it could be less, but with a few sales under my belt I'll have pretty reliable figures to work from. So £60 gross profit, minus £3 listing fees, leaves £57. Let's assume final fees at 5% of £60, that's less than £3, making my total profit £54. Across 100 listings, that's £5,400 pure profit every week, every day if I'm lucky, and much higher profits if I am really clever.

Neat tip

Calculate eBay and PayPal fees for every listing and know exactly how much you'll make from every sale.

There's a great free programme that allows you to key in eBay starting fees, initial bidding price, Buy It Now prices, and other essential features of your listing and calculates eBay listing and final fees as well as PayPal costs.

Find it at:
http://www.netoutpost.f2s.com/auction/

Benefit from my research

What should I sell, which items are most likely to attract £20 plus pure profit?

Excluding some categories featuring mainly low priced products and others with comparatively low visitor rates, if I were to focus on Sporting Goods, these are the products I'd test first.

Camping
Tents.

Canoeing and Kayaking
Canoes, inflatables, kayaks.

Cycling
BMX bikes, car racks, road bikes, electric bikes,

folding bikes, racing bikes, tandems, touring bikes, tricycles, other road bikes.

Equestrian
Bridles, horse trailers and horse boxes, saddle accessories and numnahs, saddles, rider clothing and accessories (especially designer types), riding boots, stable accessories.

Exercise and Fitness
Cardiovascular equipment, exercise bikes, rowers, stair machines and steppers, trampolines, treadmills, walkers and ski machines, abdominal exercisers.

Fishing
Boats, reels, rods. Boats and boat accessories, tents and shelters, umbrellas.

Football Shirts
One-off, hand made, famous owner, autographed, Premier Division shirts. 'Football Boots' and 'Football' are among the currently most searched for items on eBay (go to http://pulse.ebay.co.uk, in the categories box half way down screen highlight 'Sporting Goods').

Golf
Golf bags, golf carts and trolleys, electric powered trolleys, manual and pull trolleys, other golf carts and trolleys, golf clubs, full club sets, club sets with bags. Golf currently accounts for four of the top ten most searched for items in the Sporting Goods category. Current most frequent search terms in descending order: golf clubs, golf, Callaway golf clubs, golf balls.

Paintballing
Tickets, paintballing days.

Scooters
Electric scooters, petrol scooters, parts and accessories.

Scuba and Snorkelling
Dry suits, under suits, cameras and camera accessories, masks and snorkels, cylinders and tanks.

Skiing
Ski suits (especially designer types), luggage bags and racks.

Snowboarding
Snowboards, snowboard bags and rucksacks.

Snooker and Pool

Pool tables, snooker tables.

Surfing
Bodyboards, longboards, surfboards.

Swimming
Swimming pools, swimming pool equipment.

Table Tennis
Tables and Table Accessories.

Waterskiing and Wakeboarding
Jetskis, wakeboards, waterskis.

Windsurfing
Windsurfing boards, windsurfing harnesses, windsurfing masts, windsurfing sails, windsurfing sets.

Benefits of Specialising

• **Someone specialising in one or two specific sports gains** experience faster than another selling a large selection of different items over the entire range of Sporting Goods categories. Specialists can more easily answer questions from prospective buyers and ultimately achieve more sales. Buyer confidence is high for someone with ready knowledge on a subject than another who offers to research the question and answer later.

• **There's every chance of regular buyers for complementary goods** and others requiring constant replenishment compared to sellers offering hundreds of one-off products across dozens of different sporting goods categories. So there's more chance you'll be remembered as 'The golfing seller', 'The woman with the football shirts', and similar.

• **Visitors with a specific item in mind feel more comfortable checking through long eBay listings** of items relating to their particular sport than having to wade through hundreds of other products for sports that don't interest them to eventually find items they might want to buy.

• **Better chance to brand your business, make it instantly recognisable and memorable.** You can be 'Golf Balls Unlimited' for example, meaning more to golfing enthusiasts than 'Simon the Sports Specialist' who stocks all manner of sporting goods and actually has far more golf balls in stock than his better named counterpart, only too few people know it.

• **Fewer suppliers needed by sellers of one product type or tight niche market than for companies offering items across a wide range of sports**. Many manufacturers and suppliers specialise in numerous designs of one or more different items. So a firm making trampolines might make indoor varieties, huge sports hall contraptions, trampolines for toddlers, trampolines for Olympic heavyweight athletes. The firm making saddles makes dressage saddles, western saddles, side-back riding saddles, and more.

• **Bigger discounts possible for buying** – or drop-shipping – in bulk.

• **One or a handful of templates lets you upload hundreds of same-kind or similar products each week.** No need to create new templates for hundreds of different, unrepeatable products. Say you have ten different football shirt designs, ten different colours, ten different sizes, altogether 1,000 (10 x 10 x 10) possible product combinations. You need one basic template, not one thousand to list those items. Duplicate an original template 999 times; amend headings for design, colour and size; include the appropriate picture. That should take a day or two; compared to others who'll spend weeks or months creating templates for one thousand totally different items ranging from surfing boards to fishing flies, swimming trunks to golf trolleys, shuttlecocks to bicycle pumps.

• **The best competition is no competition**, and specialists stand more chance of forming non-competing relationships with suppliers. In my business, not selling sports collectibles, because I promise to work hard at selling their products I have several suppliers offering me sole selling rights to their products on eBay.

More wonderful ideas

• **The Beauty of Want It Now**. Go to Want It Now, click through, choose 'Sporting Goods', open up, and currently you'll find 1883 listings for products you could source right now. Listings having the highest number of postings are also among the most regularly visited sections, double proof of these being great sports for you to consider. These are the current number of postings by category in eBay UK Want It Now for 'Sports Collectibles':

Golf (258)

Equestrian (253)
Cycling (248)
Fishing (231)
Football Shirts (109)
Football (106)
Exercise and Fitness (105)
Camping (86)
Hunting (42)
Sailing (40)

Study your specialist area daily, not only for ready buyers, but also to keep up-to-date with items people want to buy which few sellers are currently offering.

• **Affiliate Programmes.** We've considered sourcing products from affiliate programme suppliers, while also emphasising that eBay prohibits listings for pure affiliate based schemes. The contract is between buyer and seller, not between buyer and affiliate company with seller as go between. It's easy to see why eBay bans pure affiliate product listings. But there are many ways to promote products belonging to affiliate programme supplying companies, without breaking eBay rules. The easiest way is to locate affiliate companies by direct research or via affiliate programme portals like www.affiliatewindow.com, select a few companies, contact them direct, request permission to pay personally for goods outside the affiliate ordering process. Suggest you cut the normal affiliate commission from prices you pay and ask that products go directly to your customers. You might also create a web page of links leading to affiliate products to interest your eBay buyers which you then promote via emails or compliments slips or letters sent to buyers.

• **Vintage Sporting Goods.** Most vintage and antique sports items belong more appropriately under 'Sports Memorabilia', but there's good reason to consider listing certain items in both categories, i.e. Sporting Goods/Sports Memorabilia. A good example is football shirts which can be new or second hand, mass manufactured or one-off, once worn by Pele or Beckham or the kids from the local high school, produced last week or hand-made nearly one hundred years ago. There can be a fine line between an item that's made to be used or worn, and another designed to be cherished and saved for posterity. Where category is uncertain, use both. Another reason to use both categories, especially for high value items, is to achieve maximum recognition from keyword searches by potential buyers.

So a site wide search for 'football shirt' will find you whatever your chosen listing, unlike the same words keyed into 'Sporting Goods' where you chose 'Sports Memorabilia'.

• **Do Something Different**. Offer more exciting products, like Paintball Weekends, Football Lessons, Golfing Holidays, especially at Christmas, Father's Day, Valentine's Day, and other gift-giving seasons. Such items are frequently found via affiliate companies as well as others advertising in local and regional publications in the run up to major anniversaries and celebrations. Contact these companies, ask if they market on eBay, if they don't offer to market their products on commission. Negotiate commission to cover fees for listing and finishing prices, PayPal or other payment fees, and a good profit for you.

• **Study eBay's main sellers of Sporting Goods**. These are the ones listed on eBay's Pulse Pages. Study them, check out their chosen products, learn from their listing techniques, but don't copy too closely or you risk being banned from eBay. Currently the biggest are:

fishingandfliesltd – 1095 listings for fishing flies, rods, and other fishing equipment.
warriors_world – 1254 items for martial arts, exercise equipment, handful of non-related items.
icon_martial_arts – 1200 plus listings for martial arts clothing and equipment.
lauriesed – 923 items, mainly cycling-related but some rock climbing equipment too.
buy2fish – 811 items all fishing related.

Special: football shirts old and new

They're among the very best sellers on eBay, though the market is very competitive. That doesn't mean you won't make money selling football shirts, it just means you have to be different, more careful, a better marketer.

These tips will help you get your share of this massive market.

• **Specialise within the overall football shirt category**. Football Shirts are sub-categorised by size, with lots of keyword search options, some appealing to the masses such as premier team shirts (keywords; Liverpool, Arsenal, West Ham, etc.). But there are some tiny niche markets to consider, with fewer but more eager buyers, such as Asian Teams, baby size football shirts. These smaller areas are those most likely to attract heavy bidding and high finishing prices, alongside plentiful second chance offer potential.

• **Sell anything and everything football shirt related:** old shirts in 'Sports Memorabilia' and new in 'Sporting Goods'. Be THE place to turn for shirts of all different makes, styles, ages, prices and status.

• **Watch out for fakes and unauthorised reproductions.** Fakes are usually poor quality; and unauthorised reproductions, like fakes, are illegal. Either will get you banned from eBay and could find you facing heavy fines for breach of copyright and trademarks. Some companies openly admit their items are reproduction or copies, others don't. Either way you don't want to sell anything but genuine, quality items from authorised suppliers. If in doubt, do a Google search for manufacturers and suppliers and check comments from dissatisfied buyers. There's no doubt about it, if a company isn't bona fide you'll find plenty of mentions in forums and scamfinder web sites. Visit eBay's selling forums which also feature heavily in supplier recommendations and warnings. You'll find it all at: http://pages.ebay.com/community/boards/index.html

• **Find one-off, highly collectable shirts at specialist sporting goods auctions.** Pay regular visits to www.invaluable.com, search for football shirts, and you'll find regular suppliers listed alongside others selling wide-ranging collectibles. Make a note of auctioneers' web site addresses, visit regularly, study catalogues, and you'll never miss a vital sale.

• **Look for really unusual, novel products, such as those I found from northern supplier TOFFS** – the Old-Fashioned Football Shirt Company (eBay ID: tofs04). I interviewed the company years ago, for a business opportunity magazine, and discovered a fabulous source of vintage style reproduction football shirts for major national and international football teams. There's scope for more firms to enter this novel area, without breaking copyright laws, and bearing in mind there's no copyright on ideas.

• **Look for quality items from auctions selling liquidated stocks**, overmakes and catalogue returns, where goods are normally in good condition but lack their original packaging.

Buy sports clothing and sporting goods in bulk at auction for a fraction of their market value

Auctions are a terrific source of goods, including clothing and accessories for most major sports, such as high interest eBay categories: golf, cricket, walking and rambling, running, tennis. Football shirts are particularly prolific, coming mainly from overmakes and catalogue returns.

Most lots fall into three main categories:

Liquidated Stocks: Often sold by the Official Receiver.

Overmakes: Usually direct from factories or manufacturer, sometimes wholesalers and job lot specialists.

Catalogue returns: Typically from well-known catalogue companies like GUS, Littlewoods, Empire.

Most sales are to recoup manufacturing costs, rather than to make a profit, so buy carefully and you'll always make money.

Tips to help you bag a good deal

- **Most large volume suppliers deal with larger city auction houses than smaller salerooms.** As a rule, the big city auction houses tend to sell items on a regular basis. Look in *Yellow Pages* under 'Auction Rooms/Auctioneers and Valuers', contact city-based auctioneers not small companies in small towns and villages. These smaller companies may sometimes sell sports goods but they're usually irregular, small size offerings.

- **You need to bulk-buy** – you can't cherry-pick handfuls of what personally takes your fancy. Buy in bulk and discounts can be up to 95%.

- **Check stocks whenever possible or make allowance for some faulty goods**. You'll often find that factory and wholesalers' stocks are in perfect condition, although stocks from smaller retail outlets can come through in a damaged state. People forced into bankruptcy can be disappointed and bit-

ter and is not wholly unknown for them to damage stocks rather than let someone else profit from them.

- **Pay careful attention to overmakes**. They can be the riskiest of all types of stock. They become available because a manufacturer (or sometimes an importer) has over-made (or over-bought) clothes they now have difficulty selling. That means they probably won't sell for you. Overmakes are surprisingly common and happens often when a wholesale or a retail customer cancels an order or closes down and cannot pay for it. The stocks are then put through auction to generate some cash quickly. Again, the key to successful buying is to check the stocks closely if possible. In theory, these should be perfect-condition goods. However, orders are sometimes cancelled because early-produced sample stocks are not up to the expected standard. Also, it is not unknown for manufacturers to mix in some faulty and otherwise impossible-to-sell stocks to make up the numbers and get higher bids.

- **Learn the lingo on catalogue returns;** most items are returned because the customer does not like them or they do not fit, very few are returned as damaged or faulty. Consequently some very good bargains are possible here. Most catalogue companies divide these returns into categories according to quality – typically:

   A for perfects

   B for unused (and therefore perfect) returns

   C for used (and therefore possibly not perfect) returns

   D for faulty and/or damaged stocks.

Note that categories and grading descriptions vary between companies and sometimes stocks get mixed, intentionally or unintentionally. Check very carefully or don't bid at all.

- **When bidding** (especially on goods you've not been able to check), always budget for some wastage, say 10% to 15% of items. Some goods – clothes with loose stitching, typically – can be tidied up and used or sold easily. But others – with stains, missing buttons (too much trouble to find an exact match), and broken zips etc – are of little use other than spares.

- **Stick with mainstream items** in middle-of-the-road sizes where possible and you'll rarely be left with unsaleable items.

DVD, Film and TV, Music

Consumer entertainment products are among the most successful sellers of all, probably the most profitable, too, and great places to begin your eBay venture, subject to reservations you'll hear about soon.

You'll be looking to sell under one or two separate eBay categories, namely 'DVD, Film and TV' and 'Music'. Each category has thousands of listings across a vast range of sub-categories.

This is a highly competitive market, demanding a thoroughly organised approach to selling, and almost certainly you'll work longer and harder than eBayers selling outside these categories. But the potential rewards are staggering and well worth considering as a business in its own right or as just part of your overall eBay endeavours.

I thought not to include this area in *eBay Confidential*. Lots of competition can be daunting, even frightening, but our readers are made of sterling stuff and many specifically requested this information, some intent on starting small, other choosing to go big time right away, most viewing entertainment products as a tiny part of their overall business strategy. So here it is.

The facts speak for themselves, as I discovered:

• **The marketplace is dominated by a few really big PowerSellers**, competition is rife, it's difficult to gain a foothold in the market unless you find a niche to dominate* or invest heavily in time, energy and capital. Don't panic: *they* had to start somewhere, so can you.

• **eBayers listing tens of thousands**, some hundreds of thousands of products, will earn big discounts from wholesalers, unlike the inexperienced newcomer, on a budget, who'll pay the full wholesale price.

• **Those big discounts mean resellers can undercut many other eBayers' prices** and win most of the

orders.

• **Low profit margins for sellers large and small**, mean achieving high stock turnover purely to survive. In short, if you're not prepared to 'stack em high, and sell 'em cheap' this business might not work for you.

• **The exception to the 'stack 'em high**, sell 'em cheap' rule is where you locate a niche market or sell used, limited edition and collectable items, one-offs perhaps, purchased at auction, boot sales, from collectors. This is where I recommend you begin the business.

Learn from the big players

Categories 'Music' and 'DVD/Film/TV' account for many of the world's top PowerSellers.

Take a look at http://pulse.ebay.co.uk and you'll find two of the UK's top five PowerSellers specialise within one or both of those main categories.

They are:

drsteview

gowingstore

Here's what I discovered about these major sellers:

Drsteview has almost 11,000 items listed right now and sells over 2000 items each month. He (or she) has over 10,000 DVD, Film and TV items, 196 under Music, and hundreds more listings for Mobile and Home Phones; Books, Comics and Magazines; Computing; Health and Beauty, and other.

Gowingstore currently has 7850 items listed and sells around 6067 items each month. He (or she) specialises in DVDs, CDs, PC Games, with all titles categorised and grouped alphabetically. Look carefully and amongst those thousands of listings you also find EIGHT for Fragrances and EIGHTY SEVEN for posters and calendars. A strange combination, but a good idea, and almost certainly meaning the seller has found a profitable market that's too good to miss (namely fragrances and posters). Or perhaps it's to safeguard himself against any possible slump in the entertainment market! Good idea.

The point is, these two major PowerSellers specialise overwhelmingly in Music, DVD, Film and TV, while not ignoring the wider market place.

Tips

• **Choose a niche within one or both overall categories 'Music', 'DVD, Film and TV', and dominate that niche.** There are thousands of niches to choose from. For 'Music' there's Cassettes (Christmas/Seasonal, Dance, Country, and many more); Music Memorabilia (The Beatles, Bon Jovi, Celine Dion, and more); CDs (Folk, Eminem, Trance, and more). You are spoilt for choice for niche markets.

• **By nature, niche markets mean listing fewer items than when tackling an entire category.** But niche markets are highly responsive and invariably end in more high profit sales per number of items listed than for general and mass market listings.

• **Start small and add more listings when time and money allows.** Let your business grow naturally, don't force it or you'll make costly mistakes.

• **There are companies offering Product Feeds which basically means titles and descriptions for their products are provided in a format that can be imported directly into eBay.** It saves time, but also means potentially unlimited identical listings scattered all over eBay and no chance to distinguish your business from countless others. Personally I'd rather list items individually than import products in bulk this way. That said, there is one good supplier I use and trust. That company, 'A2Z Cds', has fast changing titles, and provides information on a type of spreadsheet that allows users to create their own titles and descriptions, provide their own graphics, all before the list is imported.

Collectibles

Fast food freebies

Find a Fortunes in Freebies. Turn every Sunday morning into a profit-making extravaganza by visiting your nearest boot sale, looking for gifts and packaging from fastfoods like McDonald's and Burger King. Some are valuable collectors' items, worth hundreds of pounds and frequently offered as worthless junk at boot sales and flea markets. Keep items in their original packaging (it can more than double resale value). Don't stick at just toys; America's first Happy Meal cardboard boxes (c1979-81), with toys, are worth several hundred pounds each. Expect boxes on their own to fetch upwards of £100. Expect even higher resale profits on series of toys which fit together in puzzle form... Store in paper bags (not plastic which sweats, stains and fades colours), keep away from strong heat and sunlight which also fades colours and melts plastic.

Sea, shipping and naval memorabilia

Shipping memorabilia is one of the most consistent and fastest growing collecting areas on eBay, covering Royal and Merchant Navy, Private and Commercial Shipping.

Demand is high for most seafaring items such as postcards, photographs, menus, diver's helmets, sextants, boarding tickets, napkins rings, and more – but especially items linked to rare, unusual and tragic events.

We've bought fund-raising postcards for Titanic victims and their dependants for 10p at boot sales and flea markets and sold on eBay for £50 each. At Tyneside Metro Station last Sunday a box of 100 plus postcards of UK warships were priced at less than £1 each. I began sorting through, blocking access to other items the man had selling, when he said: 'Why don't you have the whole lot for a fiver?' Why not indeed!

I also purchased more than 200 shipping titles at an auction in Darlington. These things are much like house deeds highlighting ownership, mortgage commitment, specifications and encumbrances. They cost me £1 each plus VAT and auction buyer's premium and sold quickly at £15 per item at local flea markets, long before eBay even existed. Today I see those exact same things reaching double and triple figures on eBay. Better still, they crop up regularly at high street auction houses especially close to sea ports like Sunderland, Newcastle, Portsmouth. Keep an eye open for local auctions selling seafaring and Naval memorabilia. You'll find them advertising in local and regional newspapers, usually at the weekend.

Don't get scammed – forgeries are fooling the most experienced shipping collectors, especially Titanic memorabilia and other vessels labelled as belonging to their infamous counterpart. These tips will help:

- **Check the history** – provenance in the trade – of items offered for sale, how they were acquired, when, how they were authenticated, who says they are genuine, and so on.

- **Check inscriptions against purported age of the item** – ink fades, paper discolours and foxes – both are hard to fake.

- **If paper is pristine, ink clear, printing pure** – be suspicious and seek advice from major auction house ephemerists – contact Christie's, Sotheby's, Phillips, Trevor Vennett Smith, all listed at www.1st-in-auctions.com/MajorAuctions.html

- **Expect silver and other metal engravings to lose definition,** compared with recent engravings which are typically deep, clear-cut, without blurred edges.

Come back down to earth – and remember the Titanic is just one of thousands of collectable shipping themes. Titanic items might fetch thousands of pounds, but they're harder to find, so focus on less-well known ships, such as passenger liners, warships, merchant vessels. They're still big money-makers – for example a Union Castle passenger ship sugar bowl is worth about £70, the bell from the submarine which sank the Lusitania is worth £14,000, and memorabilia from little-known ships on uneventful journeys can still fetch £100 to £500 each, especially from collectors in their area of origin – easy to find on eBay even thousands of miles away.

Model trains and railways

Model train enthusiasts come in various guises, from collectors of items originally designed as toys (with or without moving parts); to scale model enthusiasts whose main interest is rare, vintage, working models appealing more to adults than children.

Well-known toymakers like Bing or Marklin attract the highest prices at auction.

A well-preserved toy can fetch spectacular profits. Most toys were heavily used so perfect specimens are extremely rare, unlike scale models designed for collecting and cherishing. So expect perfect toys in their original packaging to fetch the highest prices.

Hornby is the name to follow for scale models with high resale potential. It's also the name to look for on the world's most collectable engines and carriages, tenders and stations, bridges, track and landscaping features.

Whoever the maker, look for famous-name trains and expect them to be worth three or four times the price of less familiar subjects. For example, a 5 inch gauge model of the Welsh Quarry 0-4-0 tank locomotive No. 1, made by S. F. Price, fetched £2,400 at Christie's, who also sold a Tyrer-made gauge model of Stephenson's Rocket for a staggering £1,500, against a meagre £120 for a gauge model of an Italian Railways express coach and a paltry £110 for a Hornby gauge clockwork train set.

Beat the experts to the best buys at boot sales and small rural auction houses. Few have experts to spot and value rarities, so expect to pay just a few pounds for items you can sell at ten or twenty times more on eBay or at specialist sales of trains and model railways.

For the biggest profits look for items in good condition, in their original boxes, limited editions, incorrect colour shades.

Maps

A map published in 1507 and one of the earliest known attempts to trace the geography of the New World – America – and the Pacific Ocean has sold at

Christie's of London for £545,600.00. The map printed by Martin Waldseemuller in 1507 and responsible for giving America its name set the highest price ever paid for a single map at auction.

Maps are a favourite seller of mine and some great bargains can be found at local auction houses that often attract little interest from book and map dealers.

Out of the way auction salerooms, some poorly advertised, especially those selling complete house contents, are my happiest hunting ground. In pre-television days, people did a lot of reading, the rich were often educated at home. Consequently many big estate clearances contain books in abundance for selling in their own right or for dismantling into prints, articles, photographs and maps.

I have found complete early sets of encyclopaedias which were packed with full page and some folded maps. It's not uncommon to pay £3 or £4 for a massive bound volume of beautiful maps, sometimes hand coloured.

These tips will help you find and profit from maps available in abundance, if you know where to look:

• *Encyclopaedia Britannica* – those printed from 1903 to the mid 1920s are usually packed with maps. The best I ever found was one of their exclusive maps-only encyclopaedias. Containing 140 plus maps, a 1903 copy cost me £3 at a local auction, and a good few maps sold for £20 and more. Nothing went unsold, even those that went unsold over several listings when bundled together in regions – Asia, American States, Europe – sold next time out for £9.99 to £29.99 apiece.

• **Inter-war economy issues used thin paper and light printing**, very unattractive compared to their 1903 counterpart. But few people want to cart inter-war encyclopaedia sets home – some sets contain 20 plus volumes – and can often be bought for pennies. Last year in Newcastle I bought an entire 1926 set of *Encyclopaedia Britannica*, containing dozens of maps, some black and white and quite plain, some big and bold and really quite beautiful. They cost me £10 in total and sold from £1.99 to fifty pounds per map.

• **The real beauty of maps in book and encyclopaedia format is that one template can be created to suit all items.** You enter details specific to most

items, such as size, origin – the book they came from, age, starting price, and so on. Even the title can be generic, for example 'COUNTRY Rare Vintage Map 1936' with only the country name to vary between listings. Duplicate the template according to how many maps you have. Now open a template for each map, change COUNTRY to actual country name, amend the eBay category according to geographic area, add the appropriate picture, upload and start on another map.

• **Theme featured maps are hugely collectable**, such as *Hobson's Fox Hunting Atlas* of 1880 that recently fetched £300 at an auction in Durham; a composite set of twelve postcards from 1906 which fitted together jigsaw style into a map of Dorset. Such thematical and regional delicacies are still found lurking at local auction, even at boot sales, and fetch high prices on eBay.

• **Promote your best maps on and off eBay**. For the Dorset composite postcard set – yes I was the winning bidder – I wrote to editors of Devon and Dorset newspapers, telling them about the item, with a great picture for their publications and, of course I mentioned they would soon be selling on eBay. Thought I can't remember the selling price, I do recall being rather pleased with results.

• **Road and cycling maps, so popular in Victorian times**, are also good sellers on eBay, often fetching ten or twenty pounds apiece. The good news is those items are often available in bulk at local auction sales. They rarely cost more than one or two pounds each.

• **Ambitious readers**, keen to break the $1 million dollar record, will do well to look for maps by maker's name, especially Speed, Ortelius, Jansson, Valk, Sanson, Homann, Freyre whose creations regularly fetch thousands of pounds at auction.

Jigsaws

Cash in on a fast-growing collecting fad and face little competition from dealers. Jigsaws are one such product which are rarely found intact and deter most bidders. They can be bought for pennies at auction, and sell for £10 or more on eBay, especially with famous names like Raphael Tuck and Sons and Chad Valley. Advertising jigsaws are particularly collectable and potentially very valuable. For example, a set of 5 Spilsbury 40-piece puzzles in a custom cabinet sold recently for £17,000. Less pricey, but still collectable, some pre-1900 wooden complete designs fetch £200 plus, especially triangular and circular designs. Buy whatever puzzles are offered at auction – except heavily damaged or obviously incomplete... Boxes are normally sealed to prevent spillage and loss – you'll rarely get the chance to check inside... Because they'll sometimes go cheap, if only one in ten puzzles survives intact, you'll still make money... Choose a quiet time and complete unsealed jigsaws on-site – remember to dismantle finished puzzles or risk someone else cashing in on your hard work... Learn more about jigsaw puzzles – they're predicted to rise in value fast – read *British Jigsaw Puzzles of the 20th Century* by Tom Tyler (£22 including p&p from Richard Dennis Publishing or locate it on amazon.com).

Automobilia

It's one of the biggest, most profitable collecting areas, involving much more than old cars and vintage spare parts. Automobilia describes numerous collectibles relating to cars, including: car mascots (big, big sellers on eBay), lamps, brochures and catalogues, postcards and ephemera, vintage models and more.

It's a popular selling area with currently 30054 entries under Collectibles>transportation>automobilia 30054 on eBay.com, against 901 under Collectables>transportation>automobilia on eBay UK

Incidentally, that isn't a spelling mistake in the last paragraph; eBay.com really does call its category collectibles with an i, while in the UK it's collectables, the latter is wrong.

Those few listings are just the tip of the iceberg because hundreds more items of automobilia are categorised elsewhere, under vehicle makes for specific car badges, for example; under keyrings, toys, mascots, and other specific product types.

With so few listings in the UK, 'automobilia' currently lacks sub-categories, unlike its .com counterpart which currently boasts 30 plus categories, some with most listings than the entire UK section for automobilia.

Current sub-categories – and these are the products you must look to find – include:

Antenna Toppers
Badges
Books and Manuals
Brochures, Catalogs
Calendars
Clocks
Clothing, Hats
Decals, Stickers
Dishes, Cups, Mugs
Gas Pumps, Fueling System
Hitch Covers
Hood Ornaments, Emblems
Horns, Bells
Hubcaps, Hub Nuts
Keyrings
License Plate Frames
License Plates
Lighters
Magazines
Original Photos
Patches
Pins
Posters
Press Kits
Prints
Signs
Spark Plugs
Steering Wheels, Knobs
Traffic Lights, Signals
Watches
Other Automobilia

Automobilia is a truly global collecting area representing a fabulous opportunity for obtaining items that few people want and which sell inexpensively in one country but are best sellers and fetch sumptuous prices elsewhere.

A good example is postcards, showing such as a close up American manufactured car which will most likely attract more US than UK or other country bidders. I say 'most likely' because there are exceptions and all depends on actual bidders on the day. In such a case I'd list my postcard on eBay.com rather than .co.uk.

Another good exmple is Bonzo Dog, on the car mascot I bought the other day. UK cartoonist George Studdy created Bonzo in the early 1900s as a character in newspapers and books and to illustrate countless gifts and household products. Bonzo is popular all over the world but generally attracts the highest prices from UK bidders. Collectors of Bonzo, and other tight niche market collectibles like stamps, postcards, Felix the Cat memorabilia, and thousands more, will search worldwide for their favourite collectables, so most can be listed on eBay.co.uk and still attract worldwide bids. This is because serious collectors will search eBay using theme name, not specific item or category.

It's important to take care choosing your country listing site.

Study 'Most Watched Listings' for popular best sellers on other country sites, notably UK and USA. Go to http://pulse.ebay.co.uk and http://pulse.ebay.com

In the categories box left of screen, choose Collectibles (Collectables in the UK), then Automobilia. In the USA dig deeper and choose a sub-category under Automobilia. Scroll to bottom of screen to view the currently most watched listings.

Today in the UK they include:

Vintage Hand Cranked Petrol Pump
Old Michelin Man
Mclaren F1 Rear Metal Enamel Badge 'Mclaren'.
Mclaren F1 Rear Metal Enamel Badge 'F1'
Mclaren F1 Enamelled Pin Badge
Mclaren FI GTR Rear Metal Enamel Badge 'GTR'
Mclaren F1 GTR Carbon Fibre Steering Wheel Centre

It doesn't take a degree in brain surgery to spot the common denominator: Mclaren memorabilia, it's attracting more visits than any other automobile collectible and indicates a great niche market with little chance of well listed items remaining unsold. 'Well listed' because quite obviously if it's badly listed, can't be found by interested parties, it might go unsold. More about this later.

To save you looking currently the most watched item of automobilia in the US is gas pumps.

Trading tips

• **Look for low cost items attracting little interest in one country which might be best sellers elsewhere**. Those gas pumps are a good example, and a bad one too, because gas pumps attract huge interest in America, but delivery could be a problem.

• **Best places to find automobilia are boot sales and swapmeets**, especially those held exclusively for collectors and others interested in old cars, spare parts and motoring memorabilia. You'll find lots of information and a diary of swapmeet events at www.showbus.com

Other Swapmeet Sites

Model Automobiles: http://www.zeteo.com/mar/swapmeet.html
Models General Including Automobiles: http://www.modelcollector.co.uk/content/diary.htm
Custom Car Swapmeets: http://www.customcar-mag.co.uk/cgi-bin/show.cgi?d=events_diary
Car Club Swapmeets: http://www.torquecars.co.uk/street/club-url.php

Special feature: car mascots (Americans call them 'hood ornaments' and 'emblems').

Car mascots were made for screwing on top of car radiators and can fetch fantastic prices on eBay, especially those from luxury cars, the Rolls Royce 'Flying Lady', for example, and others with alternative collecting appeal, like Bonzo, Mickey Mouse, Felix the Cat.

The trick to buying car mascots for sale is to keep careful records of previous realisations and to carefully study the condition of items for sale. A tiny mark or blemish can make all the difference between a mascot fetching several hundred pounds at auction or going unsold.

The earliest types were made from brass or bronze and other long-life metals. Glass was also used for really fragile specimens which were in themselves stunning works of art. Amongst the most highly prized glass types is Lalique, the most expensive and most collectable, followed by Red Ashay and Sabino of Paris.

Tips

- **You have to speculate to accumulate with car mascots**. Most auctioneers realise their value and even higher prices are possible at local auction than on eBay. But not always. At small, out of the way salerooms, I've seen highly collectible mascots, in superb condition, go for a tiny fraction of similar items already sold on eBay. I pick up what I can, keep what I fancy, but generally you may have to spend £200 to make £300. Not a problem if you know your market well.

- **Pay careful attention to prices achieved on eBay**, keep records of maker, material, any signature, age. Keep your list close by at auction, at boot sales, swapmeets, and other buying events.

- **Because you are specialising in high value items with wide appeal and huge potential profit margins**, you should spend much longer researching and learning about your product than someone selling low value items or common-a-garden household name goods. The key to success for car mascots, as for most automobilia, is knowledge.

- **Maker is important to resale prices as is an interesting pose for the figure depicted and intricate or otherwise clear design**. Most collectible mascots are figures, animals were most popular, followed by art deco figures of nude women, Native American men with feathered headdress, and more. Keep these names in mind on your buying expeditions: Lalique, Souest, Bazin, Lejeune (AEL).

- **Avoid items with lots of damage or with extensive loss of plating**. Even the most fragile glass mascots should be free of chips and without heavy scratches.

- **The most collectable date from the 1920s to 50s** although some later models are gaining interest on eBay.

- **Watch out for reproductions and fakes which are common but usually lack detail and are often heavier than the originals**. Note that reproduction does not always mean fake, unless the reproduction is designed to fool people into believing the item is a genuine original.

- **For a really great guide** with lots of illustrations see *Collectables Price Guide* published annually by Dorling Kindersley and which crop up often on eBay. It doesn't have to be new, any recent issue will do.

Car advertising brochures

Advertising brochures are in high demand – especially linked to another popular collecting theme, such as motoring.

Few paper collectibles have survived the decades unscathed, so prices for pristine specimens regularly break records at auction. For example, 1950/60s sales brochures for cars sell anywhere between £8 and £200 depending on condition and rarity. Mass-produced brochures for everyday vehicles, such as Ford Anglia, Austin Mini, are worth about £5 each. Buy hey, be optimistic, I've bought hundreds of these things in massive boxes and paid just two or three pounds for the whole caboodle. Now that really is easy money. Bear in mind the chance of uploading hundreds of different items using one template requiring just a few changes each time and you'll begin to see the easy money to be made here.

Tips

- **Fewer brochures were produced for more exclusive models such as a 1950's Ferrari and are worth about £200 each**. In collecting terms 'old', therefore currently collectible, means pre-1970; but watch out, in ten years time expect 80's brochures to be worth double their current value, then 1990s, and so on. We've found bundles of 100 plus brochures at boot sales and flea markets, costing £5 which have sold between £3 and £10 each to collectors at flea markets and on eBay.

- **Avoid being conned – or just disappointed – some manufacturers are reprinting early motoring brochures to cope with demand from collectors**. They're perfect facsimiles of the real thing but not all carry reprint details. It's easy to think a brochure printed in 1998 is 50 years old – and you might be accused of selling fake brochures. So always include a disclaimer on sales materials – say 'All descriptions given with due care and attention. We cannot be held responsible for inaccuracies where we genuinely believe our descriptions are true'. Offer a money back refund as a final safeguard. Learn more about classic vehicles, determine which are most popular and consequently whose brochures are in highest demand – ask your bookseller about *Shire Publications* booklets on cars from 1950s onwards.

Teddy bears

eBay started as a collectibles only trading site since when it has grown to include hundreds of different trading categories, until now it bears little resemblance to its early days.

That said, collectibles are still among the most popular and profitable sellers on eBay, and represent a chance for anyone to pick up items for pennies at boot sales and flea markets, which transpire to be worth hundreds or thousands of pounds on eBay.

Teddy bears are among the world's most highly prized collectibles, and auction records are often broken.

The best profits come from 'miracle finds'; older, rarer bears picked up at boot sales, local auctions, and re-sold for high prices on eBay or at specialist sales.

Some prices exceed even the highest expectations, as did a uniformed teddy called Edwin sold at Phillips for £4,715 having been expected to fetch just £200. History, not maker, caused fierce bidding when it was discovered the bear had survived World War One inside the tunic of a soldier serving in the trenches of Eastern France.

Another bear with pedigree and a high selling price to match, Alfonzo, a rare red Steiff bear, once belonging to a Russian princess, went for £12,000 to an Oxfordshire man, who later paid even more for Aloysius, the bear that was the regular companion of the Anthony Andrews' character in *Brideshead Revisited*.

History aside, condition remains the most important factor determining resell value. Most teddies are meant to be played with, not cherished, explaining why any that have survived the passage of time – unscathed – are fetching considerable prices at auction.

Like most vintage collectibles, bears had a golden age, when collecting reached its peak. Well-preserved specimens from the period – 1903 to 1910 – can reach staggering sums, especially those made by Steiff, whose label spells value and style.

Teddies bearing the Steiff insignia fetch immense prices, as happened in 1993 when a Canadian couple bid £49,500 for Elliott, a blue mohair bear made by the German company for Harrods in 1908. The same year another bear went for £55,000, setting a new world record for a teddy bear at auction which was quickly overturned the following year when another Steiff sold for £110,000.

While other types are hugely collectable and profitable, including some modern limited editions, it remains the Steiff that fetches most regular major prices at auction, including eBay where many other bears, old and modern are also in great demand.

How to spot a steiff bear

You can spot a Steiff by a metal button in the left ear bearing the maker's name. A yellow fabric tag appended to the button indicates a mass-produced Steiff, white fabric indicates a limited edition. But the tag is often missing from older bears which can still be identified as mass produced or limited edition by reference to a good research guide such as those listed later.

Many modern day Steiffs are also in high demand and regular high sellers on eBay. In the past month a Steiff Limited Edition Titanic Mourning Bear, created entirely from black fur, fetched £600 on eBay, a Steiff Panda Teddy Bear from 2002 fetched £239.99, and several other limited editions from the 1950s through to the nineties sold at £200 plus.

Teddy buying tips

• **Look for modern day teddy bear makers who are creative but often poor at promoting themselves**. Find them at teddy bear fairs, through magazines for teddy bear collectors, at craft fairs. Offer yourself as their sole marketing representative. Showing how valuable modern day bears can be, three days ago, on July 7th an exclusive one only bear by Michelle Lamb (ID: oneandonlybears) fetched $2659.89, four days earlier another of her bears reached $1085.99. A pretty bear by Mary Holstad (ID: mmh3of5) fetched $1324.90 on July 1st.

• **Consider buying most older teddies** – old in age, not just condition – especially at boot sales and flea markets, particularly any with designer labels. They may not be Steiffs but they could be worth a great deal, in good condition, especially with an interesting pedigree. Ask sellers about their bears, note any interesting tales, make a big thing of pedigree in your auction listings.

• **Arm yourself with a few good books**, magazines and price guides, like:

Magazines

Teddy Bear Scene published monthly, every second Thursday, price £3.00 or available on subscription at www.teddybearscene.co.uk

Teddy Bear Club International available on subscription for £42 a year, currently on special offer at £29.99 at www.magazine-group.co.uk

Books

The Story of the Steiff Teddy Bear: An Illustrated History from 1902 by Gunther Pfeiffer, published by David and Charles, ISBN: 0715316060

The Ultimate Teddy Bear Book by Pauline Cockrill, Published by Dorling Kindersley, ISBN: 1879431068

Kitchenalia!

'Kitchenalia' – Americans call it 'kitch' – describes kitchen-, food- and drink-related items. It's a fast-growing collecting area that is attracting record prices at auction and includes bottles and condiments sets, rolling pins and scales, cookery books and milk jugs.

Such things were used daily and were often thrown away, meaning few have survived the decades unscathed.

So unusual and perfect pieces rise fast in value, like a 200-only edition World War II coffee pot in the shape of a frog which recently fetched £8,000 at auction, or Mrs. Beeton's cookery books which I've bought at boot sales and general auctions for two or three pounds and made £25 each on eBay.

These tips will help you make money from everyday household items.

• **Honeypots/Honey Pots** have inspired collectors over several centuries, for items old and new, and are hugely popular sellers on eBay. Keep your eyes open at craft fairs for locally made items. They normally cost very little and few craftsmen market well outside of local fairs and shops. Jump in fast, offer to represent them on a wider scale, on eBay. Get them to produce limited editions of their most popular designs. Limited editions command higher prices, so expect a honeypot costing £20 to be worth at least double restricted to 100 lots only. Ask your expert to add an inscribed signature and number pieces from 1 onwards. At boot sales and flea markets keep your eyes open for older designs and modern day cast-offs.

• **Salt and Pepper Shakers are hugely popular**, especially by a particular artist or maker, or having a special theme or subject. Among designers Clarice Cliff* is especially popular. For collectable characters and themes, think Disney characters, advertising and named location pieces.

• **Clarice Cliff created some of the most highly sought after pieces of tableware and other kitchenalia and is well worth studying further.** Her ceramic designs are universally popular and attract high prices from USA collectors. Items sold in sets are typically worth four times more than items sold singly or with original parts missing. For example, a Cliff honeypot minus lid is worth about £200, £900 or more complete. Rarity prompts most auction records and Cliff's more bizarre shapes and designs attract higher prices (e.g. conical shape coffee sets – one recently went under the hammer for £10,350, a United Services Cruet set, depicting brightly coloured soldier, sailor and airman fetched £977). Cliff designs were meant to be used, the idea was to brighten the table during the big Depression, and few have survived intact, so expect a big different in price between damaged and perfect items.

Learn more by joining the **Clarice Cliff Collectors' Club** (Fantasque House, Tennis Drive, The Park, Nottingham, NG7 1AE).

Recommended Reading

Clarice Cliff, The Art of Bizarre by Leonard Griffin, published by Pavilion.

Tea trays and boxed

lots

Many local auctioneers are lazy, can't be bothered to list all items individually, so they pile them onto trays, into boxes, and sell them as one lot.

Some bulk lots at auction contain hundreds of items, including valuable and non-valuable. The trick is to buy these items in bulk, split them and categorise as worthless (destined for the rubbish bin), worth a few quid (list at low, low prices on eBay), collectable (assess condition, value items through catalogues or specialist dealers, list in eBay's comprehensive Collecting categories).

Some amazing bargains and resell prices are possible. For example, at the recent sale of Dame Catherine Cookson's possessions, a local dealer purchased twenty trays packed with tiny knickknacks... spoons, paperback books, magazines, tiny ornaments, crochet doilies. Each tray costing around £25 each contained 15 plus items which next week sold individually at North Eastern collectors' fairs and flea markets at highly inflated prices.

Buy all you can this way, at best you'll sell everything, at worst you can put them back in their boxes and auction them again.

Autographs

PowerSeller Steve Chapman tells why autographs are terrific investments with high resell and alternative investment potential.

"They're easy to research and you can buy, store and sell them easily. The profit potential is substantial. Laurel and Hardy autographs, for instance, were selling at £600 a time about six months ago now they're closer to £900. There are many more similar examples."

As to which are the best autographs to buy right now, Steve highlights the following examples.

- **Queen**, the rock group, is a must-buy autograph investment. Freddie Mercury was the star but complete, four-signed items will be the price-risers. Three of the four original members are still alive. As they pass away, prices are likely to rise. The Who is another must-buy. Two of the original line-up are still alive, and prices should rise as and when

they die. Multi-signed pieces with the original drummer, Keith Moon, are the ones to go for. (**Editor:** Recently I saw a concert programme on a postal auction list, starting price £10, with all four Queen signatures. I forgot to bid. No one else bid either and the autographs were returned to the vendor! That was less than six months ago since when Queen signatures have risen to around £100 on eBay).

- **J. K. Rowling**, the Harry Potter author, is a rare signer, although I see a lot of faked autographs on eBay and other online sites. The big-money maker is to get the autograph on one of the books, preferably a first edition hardback. I've just seen a signed first edition of *The Chamber of Secrets* valued at £3,200. That'll go much higher.

- **The Apollo 11 crew** is a good autograph investment too. Neil Armstrong is a recluse nowadays and refuses to sign anything. That in itself makes a complete set of all the Apollo 11 astronauts' autographs a rarity. Prices will rise for all sorts of reasons, not least the re-awakening of US interest in the space programme. (**Editor:** A set of autographs for the Mercury Seven astronauts on photograph sold recently on eBay for the equivalent of £1,407.38 in US dollars).

- **Queen Elizabeth II** signatures are very rare as well. The main items available are official cards and letters. (**Editor:** I have actually seen lots of Christmas cards signed by her at local auctions, strangely fetching very low prices, so the resell potential on eBay is high).

What makes these autographs so profitable

These hot investments all have certain characteristics in common. If you apply these characteristics to other autographs on offer, you can judge whether they might generate high resell prices too.

- **We're absolutely talking big names** and legendary figures here like Stan Laurel not Shane Richie, Freddy Mercury as opposed to some here-today-gone-tomorrow *X Factor* runner up.

- **Rarity is important**. Someone who is an enthusiastic signer devalues their autograph. Jeffrey Archer was well-known for signing everything in sight; J. K. Rowling doesn't. If there's an endless supply of autographs, prices will never go up as demand will always be satisfied and prices will remain low.

- **The team element is important**. If you've got four or five members in a group, a complete set of autographs will always be worth more than the value of the four or five separate autographs. It's linked with the rarity characteristic: getting one signature is relatively easy, but getting the whole set is much harder. I also like the look of World Cup '66 sets of 12 autographs (the team plus Sir Alf). These are relatively rare and will rocket in price around 2006 and 2016, the 50th anniversary. (**Editor:** Recently a set of individual autographs for Bobby Moore and his fellow 1966 World Cup winning team members sold on eBay for just £799. The autographs were mounted and framed around a picture of Bobby Moore carrying the Cup and flanked by his fellow footballers. That seemed cheap to me and will no doubt rise in value even in the short term. But hey, I'm not made of money: I let that one pass!)

Trading tips

- **Buying when the market is relatively flat should ensure a buy-low price; at least in relation to what prices are possible later**. Prices tend to rise whenever the subject is in the news: the Who are touring, J. K. Rowling has a new book published, the Queen has a health scare. Buy when everything's quiet and well before any anniversaries or special events.

- **Invest in undedicated pieces where possible**. 'To Raymond' limits interest to all but the Raymonds of this world.

- **What's signed is important.** If it's a band, you'll want a signed LP or concert programme. If it's an author, it's got to be a book.

- **You really want autographs all together on one single item, not on four or five separate cards**, although these individual pieces can look wonderful and make a highly prized ornamental pieces, like the Bobby Moore photograph surrounded by team player autographs. I've also seen high prices achieved for individual autographs mounted in a frame with the person's photograph placed alongside. This sort of thing looks wonderful where individual items feature in separate apertures on the overall mount. To see how it's done visit eBayers: tour-passes, phildickens.

- **The highest prices go to rarities that also look good as with everyone signing in the same pen**, rather than three in black ink, one in blue and another with a mauve felt tip.

- **Sell when the market is at a peak so you get the best possible prices**. This generally means on an anniversary or a special event. Death is the biggest price-rising trigger of all. Take any celebrity who dies and today's price will be up on yesterday's. It can often double almost overnight. Of course, with most celebrities, that price will then fall back down. But not so much for big-name, legendary figures, like baseballer Babe Ruth whose autograph is one of the most highly-prized of all autographs sold on eBay. For people like this prices just keep going up... and up... and up!

- **Be careful of fakes flooding the market**. They are sometimes very, very hard to detect, so much so that even the experts turn to graphologists – handwriting experts – to prove the real thing from a worthless fake. Cut the risk by checking background of every autograph before buying. Look for related items that might exist alongside to prove authenticity, such as letters to and from the subject, relationship of seller to the subject (a family member might usually be trusted). Bear in mind that agents were often allowed to sign on behalf of famous people, especially Hollywood stars. Moreover, really famous people had their autographs printed onto postcards and photographs, looking every bit like a genuine ink hand-written signature. But look closely, you can often spot the real thing by the ink fading, blots and smudges in the ink, heavy handwriting causing deep impressions in the card.

- **Be prepared to be wrong sometimes**. Remember that Malcolm 'Mighty Mac' McDonald football programme I told you about last issue, the one I swore was a definite high priced best seller? Well I was wrong! It didn't fetch a solitary bid, no watchers either!

Recommended reading

The Sanders Price Guide to Autographs: The World's Leading Autograph Pricing Authority by Saffro, Smith, Sanders, Shaw, Roberts, published by Alexander Books. ISBN: 1570900949

The Official Autograph Collector Price Guide by Mary Allen Baker, published by Odyssey Publications. ISBN: 0966971094
Check out www.amazon.com for some fabulous discounts on new and used copies.

Collectors' stamps

Stamp collecting is one of the world's top collecting interests, alongside coins and postcards and represents a great business opportunity for most people, even if you really can't tell a Penny Black from a Green Shield stamp.

I've actually specialised in stamps myself, and I know a big fat O about stamps.

These tips will help you get started as a stamp dealer.

Never mind the quality, feel the width

• **Offer stamps in bundles**, by theme, not individually by value. The most expensive stamps are individual items, rare, highly prized, and they attract immense prices at auction. But they're risky investments for resellers, because stamp values fall as well as rise – a bit like Unit Trusts. Play it safe, sell low value stamps, by theme, such as Dogs, Space Travel, Concorde. Do it like this: arrange several same theme stamps on a piece of card, cover with cellophane paper or glassine bag, tape into place, sell under non-stamp eBay categories, like: Animals, Aviation, History, etc. Some eBayers specialise in bundle packs including: creativityplus4, wardstamps, mr.firswood.

• **Buy big bundles of stamps at non-stamp auctions where you'll often find massive albums available alongside envelopes packed with stamps and few trade bidders**. These lots rarely contain collectors' items, they're often dealers' unsold stocks or collec-

tors' duplicates, and they often fetch low bids, often less than £50 for thousands of stamps. It isn't worth picking over these items to sell individually, but there are two ways to make decent reliable profits:

i) Break the lot into two or more separate lots, such as all albums, all envelopes, all one country, all one theme. Add a decent profit to the proportionate amount paid for these items, include eBay fees, then use this as your Buy It Now or auction starting price.

ii) List the entire package at a price that attracts a good profit for you. Start your auction at this price, avoid Buy It Now unless you're in a hurry for money. I've seen some great prices achieved by sellers of big bundle stamp packages on eBay. Some eBay sellers specialise in buying and selling bulk stamp listings, such as: tenoclockshow, wrapandpack, city-collectables.

Let the experts value your stock

If the thought of selling high value individual stamps still appeals, here's how to get the experts to describe and value your stock:

• **Buy stamps at auction where the experts have already described and valued the stamp.** This works best when few or no dealer bidders are present and could mean the stamp goes at way below its regular resale value.

• **Some stamps, in albums**, have their Stanley Gibbons catalogue number highlighted alongside. Stanley Gibbons is the main trade and collectors catalogue and their numbers are highlighted by the prefix 'SG'. Sometimes the catalogue value is marked alongside. Bear in mind values change and the highlighted price may no longer apply. Obtain updated copies of Stanley Gibbons catalogues – there's a big choice covering All World stamps and individual country stamps, alongside other specialties. You'll find them selling on eBay.co.uk. Match the album description of a stamp with the Stanley Gibbons equivalent and use these as your description and starting price.

• **Sell stamps belonging to someone who is an expert**. Act as a trading assistant and get the vendor to describe stamps for you to list.

Problem areas

- **Make clear scans of your stamps**. Condition is important, as is postmark. What the non-expert thinks is good condition might be absolute rubbish to a collector.

- **As for all high price collectibles, fakes abound**. Even the experts are fooled sometimes, as a novice you could be tricked more often. Include something inside your listing to say you are describing to the best of your ability and that all items wrongly described are subject to a money back, no questions asked guarantee.

Places to buy stamps in bulk for bundling into theme or country packs or selling straight on eBay

eBay is a good place to start and you'll find several sellers of unsorted, unchecked stamps. Be careful, study feedback, make sure the seller really is selling stamps that haven't already been picked clean. A good way to spot a picker is to check if the seller also lists individual high value stamps alongside massive bundles. Where that's the case, avoid buying unless other buyers profess satisfaction with their bundle buys.

Firms specialising in bulk sales

Mastermix www.apexstamps.com
A J H Stamps Ltd. www.ajhstamps.co.uk
Stamp Warehouse www.stampwarehouse.co.uk

Stamp Auctions

A J H Stamps Ltd. www.ajhstamps.co.uk
Plumridge and Co. www.plumridge.co.uk

Sports memorabilia

I've seen more bidding wars between collectors of sports memorabilia than in almost any other eBay category. It represents one of the most profitable of all eBay trading categories. However, for newcomers, it is also the most confusing, too.

On the plus side, you'll find some amazing prices being paid for memorabilia that few would consider rare, certainly not unique.

For example, in the last thirty days:

- **A programme for the final day of the Open Golf Championship in Hoylake**, Cheshire, in 1947, went for £840 from a starting price of just £24.99. On 26th August a book called *Golf Architecture* by Dr. A. Mackenzie, dated 1920, fetched £385.

- **A rather bland postcard of Liverpool's Annfield football stadium from the early 1900s fetched £175**; a photographic postcard of Sheffield United's 1925 FA Cup Team reached £103, a full set of Scottish Football Soccer Gum Cards from 1963 reached £633.55.

- **A baseball autographed by legendary Babe Ruth** fetched US $4,150.00, approximately £2,255.43.

- **A letterhead from a company that made fishing reels in Nevada in the early 1900s**, this one dated 1906, fetched $104, about £57.

Finding items like these to sell is not that difficult. In fact, many record priced sports items are quite ordinary and not that rare. The high prices are purely because this is a popular collecting area with lots of eager buyers.

I wouldn't be surprised to find some of those items, and many others like them, fetching low sums in out of the way auction rooms. In fact, I've bought many such items myself, and passed on others, not realising their potential on eBay.

I've paid a few pounds for some – pennies for others. You'll find the best buying places are country auction houses, away from main transport routes, remote from major towns and cities. Best of all, these places rarely advertise their wares online or in print publications, so specialist trading visitors are rare and prices are generally low.

I've also found valuable items at boot sales and flea markets, again the most poorly promoted frequently yield the highest rewards.

Let me give you a recent example...

Yesterday I acquired a football programme signed by Malcolm MacDonald, the legendary 'Mighty Mac', one of Newcastle United's best known footballers from the 1970s. I'll list it on eBay soon; it may not fetch a fortune, but what do I care, I paid nothing for it! I actually discovered it slotted in the pages of a book of maps I bought last week at an auction in Morpeth. The book itself cost £5 and it's packed with maps dating from the early 1800s. I expect to make good money on those maps, and Magpie Mighty Mac's autograph? Or should I offer it as a programme? It doesn't really matter, it will at least cover the cost of the auction lot, of that I am quite certain!

Sports memorabilia is a trading arena well worth entering. Yet with so many sports, product types, special categories to consider, the novice seller can easily be overwhelmed.

Research this area before attempting to sell. Initial planning means bigger profits later

Take Care Choosing eBay Site and Listing Category for Highest Market Penetration

Sports Memorabilia categories vary between eBay country sites so you could face problems over what category is best for a newly acquired product that you have never encountered before. eBay.com's equivalent to 'Sports Memorabilia' is 'Sports Memorabilia, Cards and Fan Shop', and there the real confusion starts. Within 'Sports Memorabilia, Cards and Fan Shop', collectibles are classified by type, such as Autographs, Fan Apparel and Cards, rather than by individual sports title as in the UK. Vintage equipment, programmes and other early collectibles frequently go under Sporting Goods on eBay.com; in the UK that category is largely reserved for modern day items. Very confusing and your best bet is to study current and past listings for similar products and always check eBay's suggested category when you begin listing your item.

Learn the lingo and triple visitors to your eBay listings

Some sports are described by different names even on the same country site. For example, on eBay.com I found fishing reels described as of interest to anglers, fisherman, fishing enthusiasts. Which do you use? I suggest you use as many as possible in your title! Use just 'Vintage Fishing Reel', and you'll miss bidders using 'angling' as their search term, unlike 'Vintage Fishing Reel. Angling Collectible', or

similar.

- **Also confusing**, Table Tennis was once called Ping Pong, Football is sometimes termed Soccer.

- **Some sports considered unworthy of their own eBay category**, such as Table Tennis and Snooker/Pool/Billiards, are among the most highly prized postcard and ephemera collectibles. Again, check completed listings to decide how best to describe and list your product.

- **Although numerous items fall within the scope of Memorabilia**, you will find that paper and other historical items are amongst the most highly prized, hence the reason we'll cover them closely here.

Sell first on eBay.co.uk, with these vital exceptions

Sports memorabilia is a huge area, and a comprehensive introduction is well outside the scope of this article. So we'll cover the most important here and, because some sports break more auction records than others, so we've added asterisks (**) to those we consider deserving of special attention.

Don't concern yourself yet with variations in eBay selling categories, list first in the UK (subject to certain exceptions mentioned later) and grow experience before expanding to other country sites.

Listed below are the Sports Memorabilia categories currently listed on eBay.co.uk.

American football memorabilia

This entry is superfluous in my opinion because if I had items of American Football interest I'd list them on eBay.com, not on the UK site with a lower eBay membership and fewer American Football enthusiasts than its U.S. counterpart.

** Boxing Memorabilia – big name fighters and how they affect prices

A great collecting area with lots of potential bidders and high realisations for postcards, pictures, posters, programmes, and virtually anything associated with professional boxing. Championship belts and professional trophies are especially collectable. Note 'professional' because amateur personalities and events typically attract less interest, the exception being amateur later turned professional celebrities. As for most sports, certain personalities are more collectable and hence more expensive than others. In boxing, the big eBay names are: Muhammad Ali, Sugar Ray Robinson, Joe Louis, Jack Dempsey. Almost any pre-1900 named professional boxer item sells, at a premium if condition is good.

** Cricket Memorabilia: A little cricket goes a long way to bolstering your auction prices

Another hugely profitable area and virtually anything old with a cricket influence can fetch immense prices. Like some other sports, primarily football, rugby, ping pong (now called table tennis), some shocking prices are possible for otherwise ordinary items with additional cricket interest. For example, Bonzo dog postcards worth about £5 each can reach £70 or more if the subject or caption is cricket-based. The same might be expected for otherwise cheap items, such as advertisements for virtually any product featuring cricket, a topographical print featuring cricket, and so on.

** Football Memorabilia: why niche marketing pays high dividends in eBay's most popular collecting area

Football is probably the most popular sports collectible on eBay.co.uk and one with lots of sub-categories, some broken down into dozens of sub-sub-categories. As for most forms of niche marketing, by focusing on one small 'niche within a niche' you could become one of a handful of eBayers selling exclusively to a small but eager, high spending market on eBay. I've spotted people specialising in football programmes relating to one team or era, some selling keyrings with football motifs, others selling autographed football shirts belonging to well known players.

Football is a huge area, as you'll see from these first level sub-categories under Football Memorabilia on ebay.co.uk

Autographs (Original)
Autographs (Pre-Printed)
Badges / Pins
Bottle Openers
Calendars
Caps / Hats
Ceramics / Plates
Clocks
Fanzines / Journals / Magazines
Figures (Corinthians)
Figures (Other Manufacturers)
Fixture Cards / Lists
Handbooks / Annuals
Keyrings
Lighters
Magnets
Medals/ Coins
Menus
Mousemats
Mugs / Tankards
Pennants / Flags
Photographs
Postal Covers
Postcards
Posters
Prints / Pictures
Records / CDs / Songs
Rugs
Scarves
Tickets / Stubs
Towels
Trading Cards / Stickers
Trophies
Watches
Wristbands
Other Football Memorabilia

That reference to 'Postcards' presented my biggest eBay surprise this month. It explained why postcards I'd listed depicting football teams fetched low prices under 'Postcards>Sport', compared to those listed in the specialist Football Memorabilia section. In fact I didn't realise the category existed until today. It's confusing, and if, like me, you list everything using templates with categories chosen months ago, you could remain oblivious to this type of anomaly for quite some time. Maybe indefinitely.

- **Top football clubs are in very strong demand for most collectibles**. A torn, tatty, really dirty copy of Manchester United on an early real photographic postcard recently fetched over £100 on eBay. Conversely, good quality lesser known team postcards frequently fail to sell, even at a fiver each.

- **Specialist eBay football memorabilia sellers to emulate**: Mork42; Footballmad_2002

** Football Programmes – 7 insider secrets for turning bargain buys into 'must have' best-sellers

A hugely popular collectible but not without problems for inexperienced sellers.

These tips will help you gain experience fast:

- **Avoid bulk offerings of football programmes**, especially running to thousands of items. They could be recent programmes, heavily duplicated, we've even seen bulk offerings which are actually torn, tatty, wet, all-identical copies of programmes picked up from the floor at last week's match.

- **Particularly pay careful attention to bulk offerings from sellers also offering individual and rare specimens**. Their obvious knowledge of individual items means you're unlikely to find anything worthwhile in the bulk package.

- **Big bundle packages without heavy duplication could be worth buying for bundling into team and year packages**.

- **Buying bundles to sell as low price individual eBay listings is a good way to build feedback and develop selling experience**. Bundles, without heavy duplication, are also useful as shop stock or Buy It Now multiple product listings.

- **Highest priced programmes tend to come from the 1920s and 1930s or from major historical events such as England's 1966 World Cup Win**. Big teams dominate the highest realisations and theirs are the names you'll find featured in frequently searched eBay keywords (see later).

- **Autographed programmes are likely to command a premium especially for famous teams and celebrity players.**

- **eBay's Football Programmes category breaks into further selections**, any of which represents a tight niche for you to consider and perhaps even dominate. Those sections are: League Fixtures, Non-League Fixtures, Charity Shield Fixtures, F. A. Cup Fixtures, League Cup Fixtures, Scottish Fixtures, European Club Fixtures, International Fixtures, Friendly and Pre-Season Fixtures, Reserve Fixtures, Schoolboy / Youth Fixtures, Testimonial Fixtures, Women's Fixtures.

** Football Shirts – a football shirt sells every 5 minutes on eBay, be sure to grab your share

'Football Shirts' features twice on eBay: First under Football Memorabilia for old shirts, probably with well known owners or of historical significance. Second under Sports Goods where you'll find hundreds of new and lightly used shirts with lots of eager

bidders as you'll see in next month's issue where we feature football shirts old and new, from newly released club strips to vintage collectibles with past famous owners.

** Golf Memorabilia – breaking more price records than almost any other sports collectible

Like many other sporting categories, it isn't just golf memorabilia per se that fetches high prices on eBay. Add golf to almost any other collectible or consumer product and the market and bidding for that product will invariably reach new heights. Vintage playing cards, for example, with golf interest, appeal to collectors of playing cards in general and golf enthusiasts in particular. In such cases it's a good idea to consider listing in two categories: playing cards and golf memorabilia.

These tips will help you buy with confidence for this great collecting area:

- **Golf-themed postcards are hugely popular**. The earliest cards, with undivided backs – no line separating message from address – fetch the highest prices. The line dividing address from message side on postcard backs appeared about 1902, previous to which the back was reserved for the address and the message had to be written on the picture side on a typically wider border than existed later. These vintage cards are worth about £75 each. Named players are catalogued at £70 and professional tournaments fetch about £60. These are catalogue values, almost insignificant on eBay where much higher realisations are likely for postally used cards in good condition.

- **Tournament programmes are major best sellers even from as recent as the 1960s**. Earlier items with famous named players or programmes for majornational and international golfing events are regular record price breakers. You might consider buying programmes from the last twenty years or so, keep them five or six years, then list them on eBay.

- **Clubs and balls are popular collectibles especially those from the 18th century which turn up infrequently at country house estate sales**. Though still rare, 19th century items reach high prices, according to age, maker and condition.

- **Most collectible makers include**: Thomas Dunn, Tom Morris, Charlie Hunter, McEwan and Todd. A

McEwan and Todd club with leather face insert is valued in *Miller's Collectables* at £4,000 – £5000, who also value a Jackson play club with horn insert and lead back weight at £8000 – £9000. (Source: *Miller's Collectables Price Guide* published annually by Dorling Kindersley).

- **Famous owner clubs and golf balls are hugely collectable and can fetch immense prices**. They are rare and I can't find any recent eBay examples, but you'll see some amazing offline auction record breaking clubs and other golf memorabilia listed at http://www.abrexa.co.uk/p2/golf/golf-club-auction.htm

- **Advertising golf balls**, especially pre-1920, carry a premium over standard plain balls of similar design.

- **Early golf balls were feather stuffed and regularly fetch thousands of pounds apiece**.

- **Keep an eye open at auctions and flea markets for vintage prints**, especially from well-known illustrators. Prints can be separately produced or removed from books and folios. Be sure to mention the source in your eBay listing, as original print or book plate, and specify if a book plate includes other illustrations or text on the reverse. Look for prints by Cecil Aldin (Stop Press News: Aldin's prints fall into the public domain on January 1st 2006 meaning you can legally copy and sell his wonderful designs); Phil May, Louis Wain (his cats playing golf prints appeal to golfers and cat enthusiasts), Lance Thackery.

Early photographs represent another high ticket item with scope for reproducing copyright-free specimens. Original photographs of well-known players, also caddies, fetch high prices even in damaged condition, notablyfrom the late 1800s to early 1900s.

- **Also popular and attracting regular high prices:** early calendars with golfing theme, vintage golf-ball-shaped ceramics and advertising novelties, etc.

A few words about 'other sports memorabilia'

Surprisingly, some sports listed here, though not warranting their own special eBay sub-category, are amongst the most highly prized in some collecting areas, such as postcards, prints, programmes.

Athletics

A popular postcard area. In postcards look for named athletes, meetings, stadiums where prices can often top £20 per item.

Australian Rules Football Baseball

A hugely collectible area for postcards and most other collectibles, especially in the USA and this is another area I consider superfluous on eBay.co.uk. Postcards can fetch high prices, especially stadiums and named players. Big name players like Babe Ruth fetch premium prices across the range of products and collectibles. List on eBay.com to attract the highest audience.

Basketball

Another category you're recommended to avoid in preference for listing on eBay.com

Cycling

A hugely popular postcard collecting subject and hardly worth a mention on eBay.co.uk

Snooker/Pool/Billiards – **A major collecting area with regular high realisations even for damaged memorabilia**

One of most popular themes among postcard collectors and many other collectors' groups, yet not even deserving of its own eBay category. Named players make especially collectible postcards, particularly if autographed. An old postcard I picked up for pennies, featuring a snooker player whose name escapes me, looked like it has spent years folded inside a book. The creases had almost split the card into several pieces. But it was autographed and dated, about 1930s I think. I had it a while, thinking so damaged an item would never sell. It went for £60 to a Snooker Hall owner down south who considers it a great rarity. A non-winning bidder for that tatty snooker postcard asked me for a framed reprint of the original. The copy cost me £2 and sold for £20.

Great business idea: look for items attracting lots of bids for the original product, consider buying the item and creating reprints. Re-auction the original item later. Be careful to choose public domain or copyright-free items or risk heavy fines for breach of copyright and similar laws.

Other things you need to know

• **It doesn't stop at memorabilia** – modern day products are equally profitable. All popular sports appeal to buyers for countless product types, not just memorabilia or collectibles. Among the best, in my experience: cufflinks, lapel pins, mounted prints, fridge magnets, keyrings, clocks, mouse-mats, calendars, caps/hats, ceramics/plates, fanzines/journals/magazines, figurines (Pewter is popular), handbooks/annuals, lighters, medals/coins, mugs/tankards, postal covers, records/CDs/songs, scarves, tickets/stubs, towels, trophies, watches, wristbands, etc.

• **Dig deep for bigger profits.** Pay careful attention to bundles of postcards, books, prints, cigarette cards, and other ephemera available at most flea markets and collectors' fairs, especially specialist postcard and ephemera fairs. Some dealers price items according to type, such as comic postcard, theatre programme, meaning great bargains possible on sports-related items the seller has filed by collectible type rather than sport.

• **Find treasure in old books at auction and fairs.** Study prints in most very early books, especially early newspapers and magazines which were commonly bound into whole year issues. Some are packed with prints, virtually all worth a few pounds, but some worth much more. Particularly look out for *Illustrated London News* in volumes, expect to pay £100 plus for a complete year volume (well worth the money), Sphere (lots of cartoons by famous artists such as Studdy, Hassell, Phil May), Graphic, and many others. A few hours spent scouring these items at specialist book auctions, looking for sporting prints will repay you many times over. Visit sales in poor weather, when road conditions are bad, when the event is poorly advertised or in hard to reach places and expect some wonderful savings. Few dealers like to journey far for mundane items (mundane to them, not to the sporting print enthusiast) and even fewer like to work at removing prints, preferring to offload the item intact for early profits.

• **You might buy and keep items awhile until the market favours a quick sale**. For example, cricket, already a popular collecting area, might attract far higher prices on eBay.co.uk now that England has regained The Ashes and further increased interest in the sport.

• **Regularly visit eBay's Pulse Pages where you'll find most frequently searched keywords and phrases within each auction category.** Under 'Sports Collectibles' you'll currently find: Liverpool, Manchester United, Chelsea, Arsenal, Celtic, Cricket, West Ham, Boxing, Golf, Tottenham. Learn more at http://pulse.ebay.co.uk

• **Buy hot sellers close to home.** You can buy items locally and sell online for higher prices because you are reaching a worldwide audience. Car boot sales are a great place to look. Learn about your local car boot venues by taking out an annual subscription (costs £14.00) to Car Boot Calendar – http://www.carbootcalendar.com

• **The best Internet site for sports auction details**. Learn about local general auctioneers at www.invaluable.com – you won't find all auction companies listed but you will find some specialists in sports memorabilia. Launch the Auction Directory, go to 'edit' on your browser, choose 'find', key in 'sport' and you'll find those most prolific in sports memorabilia.

• **Search and Find it Fast**. I keyed 'Sports Auctioneers' into major search engines and this is what I found topping the list on Google and most others:

Mullock and Madeley, The Old Shippon, Wall-Under-Heywood, Church Stretton, Shropshire, SY6 7D

www.mullockmadeley.co.uk

Specialist auctions: sporting memorabilia, vintage fishing and tackle, most other sports memorabilia and equipment.

Fishing reels

Man has fished almost since time began and a mammoth range of fishing related objects has emerged to form one of the most popular collecting areas.

Fishing reels are especially popular, perhaps because they are easier to display and many are highly intricate and very attractive.

These tips will help you spot a reel worth thousands of pounds against another that is practically worthless.

- **Generally speaking,** reels bearing their maker's name are more popular than unnamed reels of the same vintage. Hardy is one of the most collectable of all.

- **Check to see if the item is original or has modern replacement parts added later**. Most restoration work can be spotted from the patina, newer parts being shinier and less scratched than original features. An item that has been restored is worth less than its good quality all original counterpart; and a high standard restoration usually makes a reel more desirable than its previous damaged state. Best of all is an all original item in good clean condition.

- **Be careful when cleaning reels and keep all parts separate with their correct location highlighted**. Some screws and tiny pieces are interchangeable, many are not, even on the same or identical reels.

Other fishing memorabilia

- **Fishing tackle catalogues** and user guides are also collectable, especially pre-1930s.

- **Vintage original pictures and photographs,** including prints and other ephemera are also worth buying for resale. Check original from reproduction by quality of paper and printing. Old paper was often thicker than its modern day counterparts, ink came from a bottle not ballpoint pen, much early paper shows signs of foxing rather like tiny brown patches which is almost impossible to fake on modern day ephemera and reprints. Items showing the worst signs of foxing, where huge brown blotches cover much of the surface, should be avoided on all but really rare pieces.

Recommended reading

Antique and Collectible Fishing Reels: Identification, Evaluation and Maintenance by Harold Jellison and Daniel Homel, published by Forest Park Publishing.

Fishing Tackle – Antiques and Collectables: Reference and Evaluation by Karl T. White, published by Holli Enterprises.

Feedback

The smart way to manage your all-important feedback score and gain consistently high-ratings

Ebay Feedback is the process where buyers and sellers rate one another based on actual trading experience. If the transaction is good you can expect positive feedback from buyers and sellers. Neutral feedback indicates room for improvement; negative feedback denotes an unacceptably flawed transaction – Usually!

I say 'usually' because things don't always go according to plan. Feedback is subjective – some people are more easily pleased than others, some more forgiving while some more honest.

I have seen positive feedback left by people who haven't even received their product yet, and negative from others who just enjoy being cruel or haven't even paid the seller. Jealousy, bad hair days, downright nastiness, all contribute to negative feedback which few sellers can avoid.

Positive feedback is vital for growing a business and good reputation on eBay, especially when building feedback to sell BUY IT NOW or open a shop on eBay.

Feedback – positive and negative (neutral doesn't count for % rating) is represented as a proportion of overall feedback. So the lower your feedback rating, the higher the impact negative feedback has, unlike PowerSellers with, say, 10,000 feedbacks, for whom one more negative has little or no effect.

Once feedback is given, even in the heat of the moment, it can't be changed, so a negative stays with you for life. That's more or less what eBay says, but the reality is different. Feedback can be retracted by mutual consent (learn more via 'Feedback' in your eBay account) and firms like SquareTrade – www.squaretrade.com – will mediate to remove negatives.

Among other things, Square Trade, located in the USA, mediates between parties to negative feedback. One person, usually the seller, contacts Square Trade, as a member or non-member and 'Files a Case' for mediation and feedback withdrawal. It costs $29.95 dollars with discounts for members. Membership costs vary, I paid about £50 (US$ equivalent). Membership allows you to display the SquareTrade symbol in your listings and is a great way to generate trust and confidence in your business. For feedback withdrawal you enter the date of the feedback, the other party's ID, and reason you consider retraction appropriate. This goes to the other party, via SquareTrade. The other party is invited to respond and actually sees what you have written about them, so be nice, don't get personal! Messages pass to and fro until a SquareTrade mediator considers a middle ground has been met and invites both parties to agree to feedback retraction. It's as easy as that and, if parties agree, the negative disappears a few days later. If the other party ignores SquareTrade the case goes in your favour and the negative is usually removed. Square Trade estimate about 90 per cent of negatives are removed within two weeks of a case being filed.

These are some of the reasons you'll get bad feedback:

- **Delay in sending product.** 'Delay' for some people is more than a day between paying and receiving their product, for most three or four days is acceptable. Seven days is too long.

- **Sending product badly wrapped**. Pack products carefully, using bubble wrap or padded bags. It can be expensive but you are allowed to add packing charges to postal costs.

- **Not sending product at all**. More than three negatives for this will get you suspended or barred from eBay.

- **Item not as described.** Describe items as carefully and comprehensively as possible and always include a message like: 'Item described to the best of our ability. Money back on all items with listing mistakes or errors.'

- **Not answering emails**. Often the problem isn't

yours, the other person may have spam filters preventing your email getting through, often they're just don't check before leaving negative feedback. An estimated one-third of emails miss their intended destination, mainly due to spam filters. Most PayPal letters make it through spam filters and they're rarely missed by people who've binned many of your earlier communications. Virtually everyone opens emails saying 'There's money in your PayPal account'. Poor communications can be solved by sending a small amount of money via PayPal with a message 'You have spam filters in place, contact me asap'. Or similar. Be careful, remember the recipient of money usually pays PayPal a minimum 20 pence per transaction. Not so where you partially refund someone paying you through PayPal. Do this by entering the appropriate transaction within your PayPal account, scroll down to 'refund', pay a few pennies back. The recipient won't pay but he will get your message. Don't refund by PayPal for buyers paying you by cheque or cash. They will be charged. The exception is where you send a token amount, plus PayPal charge, to the recipient. Thankfully the majority of buyers use PayPal.

- **Charging high postage and trying to make more money that way**. You can charge extra for packing and processing but be realistic. Don't charge £10 for a package costing £3 to post and £2 for packing materials. It does happen.

- **In retaliation for leaving negative feedback for other eBayers**. This is the most common reason for negative feedback and something you must learn to live with.

- **Just Because!**

You will never please them all and it isn't worth your time trying.

Getting good, avoiding bad and managing problem feedback

- **Retaliatory negative** feedback is the most worrying aspect of all for serious business eBayers who, though they know it's their duty to warn other sellers about undesirable customers, are often too afraid of incurring negatives in return. I only give feedback when it's already been left for me. In my listings and compliments slip I say: 'If you have a problem email us at *myemailaddress* and we'll sort it out right away. Otherwise, leave feedback to let us know your product has arrived in good order and we will reciprocate within 24 hours.'

• **'Reciprocate' is the important word**, and if someone leaves positive feedback we normally leave the same; if they leave neutral or negative we contact them to ask why. If we consider reciprocal neutral or negative feedback is warranted, that's what they get. To my mind it is totally, totally wrong to leave neutral or negative feedback for anyone without first trying to resolve the problem. In this case our negative or neutral feedback isn't retaliatory, it's simply to warn other sellers about the buyer's lack of care and communications skills.

• **You can pre-approve bidders**, allowing you to sell purely to individuals who have no negative feedback themselves and don't leave it for others. You might get people to email you before bidding, you check them out, you approve or bar them from bidding. Personally, I can't see the point.

• **You can cancel bids or forbid certain people from bidding**. Visit eBay's Feedback Forum for lots of advice and comments from seasoned sellers.

• **A friendly, considerate disposition, and the ability to handle difficult people**, all help avoid the 'Big N*' which can seriously damage your business. (*Negative feedback!!!).

Now let us get real, bear in mind the bigger you get, the more items you sell, the more negatives you might genuinely earn, and the more difficult people you will encounter. Be careful, considerate, communicative. Learn from earned negative feedback, try to avoid undeserved complaints, and learn to live with whatever else happens.

Pre-empting the F Word – great Ways to limit negative feedback

Negative feedback is often left out of frustration or due to the remoteness some people experience when buying online. Unlike shopping in the high street where goods are handed over immediately, usually accompanied by a friendly smile or thank you, the typical eBay customer has little idea when his goods will arrive and only rarely do sellers contact buyers before shipping their goods.

Spend time reading other people's negative feedback comments and you'll discover many commenting on slow delivery, inability to contact the seller, failure to answer emails. By far the biggest percentage come from people who grew frustrated waiting for sellers to respond to queries or answer complaints.

My first negative came on New Year's Eve, 2004, when someone queried the download site I'd given for one of my books. He emailed about nine in the morning saying he could not find the site, I answered saying the site was fine and he was probably using a search engine to find it, which won't work, would he kindly use the browser instead.

At 6pm he emailed again, this time quite aggressive, accusing me of ignoring his earlier email. Whether he failed to notice my email or had spam filters in place, I'll never know. But instead of responding right away to that second email, I decided to finish New Year's Eve dinner and get back to him later. Back online at 8.30pm, my first priority to answer this man, I discovered he'd left negative feedback just a few minutes earlier! I will be much faster to answer next time round: New Year's Eve or no New Year's Eve!

Tips to reduce negative feedback

• **Apart from selling**, I also buy postcards and other collectibles, for personal use, and these are experiences that make me think twice about leaving negative feedback while also being good ideas I use to help prevent negatives appearing for me. As well as sending my goods well wrapped with a nice hand-written note, my favourite Bonzo Dog postcard seller always sends a 5% Discount voucher for anything else bought from him within the next six months. Another seller phones the day my products are despatched and again the day of expected delivery just to make sure all is well with the transaction. I've had suppliers send sweets, pretty thank you cards, and other small gifts to accompany my order. It's all so personal, considerate, and more likely to generate positive feedback even from the most difficult of people.

- **Spotted on the Internet(http://www.hammertap.com/news/SmartMoney.htm)** "If you get an unhappy customer, a fast response is crucial – a large percentage of negative feedback comes from customers who grew frustrated waiting to hear back about a complaint. Wendy Warren, the accessories dealer, immediately calls anyone who sends her an angry message. "What can I do to make you happy?" she asks, even when she's not at fault. "It will completely defuse the situation," she says. "It's never failed me."

Changes to eBay's feedback system

Feedback is a process whereby buyers and sellers rate one another based on actual experience. Good feedback means the transaction went well, neutral indicates a minor concern, negative means something went horribly wrong and lets the buyer or seller alert others to problems they might avoid.

But what happens when a seller of previous good standing, with say 5,000 positive feedbacks, suddenly gets ten negatives all from one buyer? I have seen it happen, those red circles stick out like a sore thumb, the seller is bound to be viewed with suspicion until those negatives make it to a less noticeable part of the feedback pages.

Those negatives may have been deserved, perhaps the seller missed sending one package containing all ten items purchased together by one person. Perhaps that one buyer of ten items has just had a fight with the boss, or maybe he is jealous of the successful seller. Whatever happens, until recently, those ten

negatives would remain to blot the seller's hitherto perfect reputation. Removal has always been possible under certain circumstances, but that takes time, and sales will still be lost in the meantime.

The feedback system is highly subjective, at the mercy of the awkward few, a worry for all good sellers.

Most negatives are left out of retaliation for receiving negative feedback, out of misunderstandings, because spam filters cause communication problems. Most are left by new eBayers who either don't understand how the feedback system works, or they don't care, or they're here for the short haul and want to cause as much disruption as possible.

eBay is usually quick to react to problems confronting its top selling members but the problem of undeserved feedback has languished for years.

Then, out of the blue, a few days ago eBay announced imminent changes to the feedback system, mainly to avoid problems caused by newcomers and disruptive members.

The changes include:

- **Feedback will be neutralised where members failed to participate in issue resolution processed**. So negatives left in the heat of the moment or out of pure nastiness where one person fails to alert the other to a potential problem won't affect feedback ratings. The comments will remain however alongside a note from eBay indicating the feedback does not count towards the total score. How much better it would be if the comment were also removed, but that isn't part of the plan.

- **Feedback – positive, neutral, negative – will be removed from users who become indefinitely suspended within ninety days of registering on eBay**. Great news, given newcomers very often leave negative feedback without reasonable cause.

- **New members will be required to complete a tutorial before leaving neutral or negative feedback.** The tutorial aims to educate new members to the variety of ways that problems can be solved before undesirable feedback is given.

Scams

The Escrow scam

Escrow is a system used on eBay, and elsewhere, where the buyer gets to inspect a product before payment goes to the seller. It works where a middleman – the escrow company – takes and holds a buyer's payment until that person receives the goods and confirms acceptance, whereupon money is released to the seller.

It gives buyers peace of mind, especially on high price items. eBay suggests buyers and sellers consider escrow for items over £250 and recommends the services of www.escrow.com, while warning against other escrow companies.

Typically, the buyer will transfer credit card or other funds to the escrow service which should eventually be credited to the seller's account. Unfortunately, con-artists have targeted this market as their latest money-maker. Various escrow sites are popping up all over the place. And they are there to part buyers from their hard-earned cash.

The basic scam is as follows. A con-artist uses a stolen credit card to buy a domain name that either has the word escrow in it or is very similar to one of the big-name escrow services. They then set up a web site, copying pages from a genuine escrow web site so the fake site looks as bona-fide as possible.

The con-artist visits various auction sites, lifts details of hundreds of items up for auction and then re-advertises these at other online auction sites. All they do is amend sellers' contact details to their own. Winning bidders are then asked to make payment via the (fake) escrow web site. Payment might be by credit card transaction or electronic bank transfer, cash, or other methods. Transfers are made, money disappears to the con-artist, often based overseas, buyers lose their money and never see any goods.

Many of these escrow sites look to be run by small-time crooks rumoured to be operating in merging European countries, including Bulgaria, Ukraine and other parts of Eastern Europe.

Many such scams are almost beyond the reach of

the law and enforcement agencies will normally refer you back to eBay (or wherever the auction was listed) who will in turn prove unable to help.

You really need to safeguard yourself and knowing how to spot a dodgy escrow site is the first big step.

A major giveaway is that genuine sellers typically offer a range of payment methods; bogus sellers don't, they insist that you use a particular escrow site.

Here's how to check if the site is genuine or bogus. Go to www.google.com, enter the escrow site url in the search box mid way down the screen (http://www.etc), and click to search. A better-known site will return plenty of mentions; a here-today, gone-tomorrow fake site may not even feature in Google's directory. Note that any url can be found using the browser, even fake sites, but search engines rarely index sites of less than three months' existence. The exception is really clever scamsters who purchase expired domains already indexed with major search engines, making it essential that you follow through on the following tips.

If Google locates the url, go to the site. If it does not start with https: and/or does not have a padlock at the bottom of the screen, the site is not secure. Bona-fide escrow sites are always secure.

Most of these scam sites seem to have a dash in their name and/or end in .biz, .org, .cc, .info, .us, rather than the generally more established .com or co.uk.

Trawl page by page for giveaway signs of a hastily created site, such as poor spelling, grammar and/or punctuation.

Check whether there is a genuine street address, a landline phone number and an e-mail address; follow them up, send a letter Recorded Delivery then check a few days later to see if it's been delivered (www.royalmail.com), talk to someone, get their name, ask how long they've been running an escrow business, where they are based.

A site that's run by a bona-fide company will state its company details; check those at www.companieshouse.gov.uk for UK based genuine sites.

These sites also help establish genuine from bogus escrow sites:

http://www.sos4auctions.com
http://escrowfraud.com

These are self-help websites that lists sites that are believed to be fake.

Visit the National Criminal Intelligence Service site at http://www.ncis.gov.uk and www.met.police.uk where you'll find fraud alerts.

Why you should NEVER give out your ID or password – even if you get a threatening email from 'eBay'!

I have a confession to make. Today I did something I have warned others many times not to do – I gave my eBay User ID and password to a scamster.

This one was clever, very clever, and thankfully I realised my mistake and changed my passwords before any real harm was done. Except to my self-esteem.

I can't believe I did it! But I did, and if it can happen to me after several years trading on eBay, I reckon it can happen to anyone. Here's why:

- **Scamsters know genuine eBayers are petrified of being reported to eBay or receiving negative feedback**. The email I received went something like this: 'I haven't received my product. Sort it out right away or I'm reporting you to eBay'. I jumped to attention, read the email again, wondering what this person had bought that I hadn't posted. I even noticed the giveaway sign of a scam, namely a strange email address you'll hear about later, but even so my eyes were pulled towards a link, purportedly from eBay saying: 'Click here to view this transaction'. There was my answer, click on that link and I'd see exactly what this person had bought. And that's what I did, and as often happens legitimately *within* eBay's system, I was asked to give my ID and password, which also I did! Next page showed a Burberry sweater, something I don't stock anyway, so I thought a little longer about this person reporting me to eBay when the penny finally

dropped. My ID and password had just been given to a scamster through a link in an email which is the conman's main tool. I had just done what I have told others so many times not to do. I went quickly into my account, *via eBay's home pages this time*, and quickly changed my password before my account was violated.

- **Never, ever give your ID or password via an email** communication mentioning eBay or PayPal, NEVER. PayPal and eBay would never send emails requesting personal details direct. The only time to give your password is when you have entered your account through the companies' home pages (normally www.ebay.co.uk and www.paypal.co.uk) or via eBay's spoof-proof toolbar that's free to download.

- **The free eBay Toolbar with Account Guard turns green** when you access a genuine eBay or PayPal site and turns red when the site might be fraudulent. You can download it right of the screen on your account's main page.

- **Change your passwords often**.

- **Though it's tempting**, do not store passwords on your computer for scamsters to access via ever improving hacking technology.

- **Have your computer virus protected** and always up-to-date to prevent clever criminals accessing passwords instantly you type them into your computer.

- **A click-through link in an email can be verified as eBay related, or not**. Take the mouse, hover over the blue link, and at the bottom of your screen you'll see the url of the destination page. If it says 'www.ebay.co.uk' it probably is from eBay, anything else is a scam. *Either way, do not give passwords via an incoming email.*

- **The latest trick is to make you follow a chain of links in an email before eventually requesting your password**, by which time you're bored, frustrated, and not thinking clearly. *Yes, it happened to me!*

- **'You've Got Money'** is a common email title, allegedly from PayPal, telling you someone has just sent you cash. How much?, how much?, you can't wait to find out. 'Click here to claim it', you're told, or something similar. DON'T DO IT! Again, it's a scam and, though PayPal will send emails about incoming payment, you should never enter your account through that email, or any email. Today it might be from PayPal, but tomorrow... .....?

• **Don't expect the experts to always be right.** Though I hate to say it, I once got an email from PayPal starting out 'Dear 'my PayPal password' where ID would be permissable). Only I and PayPal knew that password. That email had come from them, mistakenly so, but it did come from them. I changed my password right away.

• **Be especially careful if others use your eBay or PayPal accounts**, as where you have staff or others help run your business. Train those people to recognise scams and change your passwords regularly, especially when staff turn awkward or leave.

• **With eBay passwords criminals have easy access to PayPal accounts** where users storing this information for easy recall later.

• **Move cash regularly from PayPal** to your bank account in case you are tricked. £200 is the maximum I accumulate to cover eBay and other expenses.

• **There's a special spoof information site to keep you updated on current scams**. Visit at: http://pages.ebay.co.uk/safetycentre/spoof.html

• **If you are conned**, make it known to spoof@ebay.co.uk or spoof@paypal.co.uk and tell us about it to so we can keep readers informed.

People divulging eBay passwords will give away PayPal passwords too, a lethal combination. It doesn't take long to order goods in your name and pay for them using your PayPal account.

A close eBay friend phoned me one day, saying her eBay account had been violated, and she insisted on telling me why. It seemed someone had hacked into her eBay account, ordered a tractor costing £3,000 on eBay, and paid using her PayPal account. They collected the tractor the same day, before the

fraud was noticed.

Few people have that kind of money in PayPal, my friend doesn't either, and apart from £350 from PayPal the rest was charged to her credit card.

Using PayPal you pay for a purchase first using funds in your account and the rest comes from your credit card details stored by PayPal.

Worse is still to come. Few people realise their accounts are violated until their own credit card payments are refused as being over budget.

Finally, when credit card payment for eBay fees fail, you get expelled.

Watch out for these latest online auction frauds

Even experienced eBayers fall foul of scams. They inadvertently buy items they may not receive, or which are fakes the unsuspecting buyer later resells on eBay. The consequences are frightening, so whether you are buyer or seller, these tips will help you avoid becoming a victim of Auction Fraud.

Tips

The Numbers Game That Could Get You Thrown off eBay. The most alarming new trend concerns identify fraud and it works like this: a new eBayer opens shop, sells all manner of fabulous stuff, high value items with low, low, low prices, like cars, computers, jewellery. This is an eBay resellers' delight, so many products to buy low and resell high! But you'll end up losing money and tarnishing your reputation forever, and even be expelled from eBay if goods you buy to resell fail to materialise. The big giveaway is: these companies do not accept PayPal, but they do have their own Credit Card Facility which you can access by phoning, emailing or by going online to give credit card details. The scam is short lived, but very profitable, because the seller does not have Merchant Facilities. But he or she does now have your credit card details which can be used to buy on and off the Internet, long before you, your credit card company, or even eBay are aware a problem exists. Though I have Merchant Facilities myself for eBay sales, I find so few people use the facility, only three of several thousand buyers this year. Moral: pay using PayPal – they offer substantial protection against fraud – or check the status of the so-called merchant facilities seller before attempting to pay. Check by sending an email asking the name of their Merchant Facilities provider and their own Merchant ID. It goes without saying that sellers too should accept PayPal payments to stimulate buyer confidence and speedier payments than where accepting just cheques and postal orders.

Buyers Shocked by Montreal Phonebook Switch. Another major scam involves sending packages to winning buyers, getting a certificate or collection by a major courier company, and sending some low value item like a ream of paper to the unsuspecting buyer. One scamster sent a copy of the Montreal phone book to the winning bidder of a laptop computer. Looking much the same size as a laptop computer the phone book was shipped by Fedex and a tracking number provided which was just enough to convince the bidder that his package was in safe hands. By the time the phone book – or reams or paper, even rocks and bricks, arrive at their destination the scamster has packed up and moved on to new hunting grounds.

There are ways to prevent being a victim yourself either as a buyer for personal or business use.

- **'Know Your Seller'**. You should always check sellers' Feedback Score. More than two negatives for a low volume seller (under 100 sales) should be investigated; less than 99% positive feedback for a high volume seller (several hundred sales each month) is worth checking.

- **But be careful!** Make sure multiple negatives are from different sources, not just one disgruntled buyer amongst many thousands who leaves negatives for multiple orders. Recently I found someone selling postcards, and was shocked to find they had 20 negatives among 100 feedback during the current month. On further inspection I found these were the only 20 negatives the gentleman had earned over six years of eBay trading and all came from one person. I checked that individual and discovered he rated every purchase he'd ever made as negative. Good enough for me, my seller was a very genuine seller, and just another sad victim of the Customer from Hell.

For more advice on knowing whether to trust your seller visit: http://pages.ebay.co.uk/help/buy/ia/trusting_the_seller.html

- Most prosecutions are based on people selling items they do not already possess and can not reliably obtain when auctions end. In a recent example, police in Kansas prosecuted a woman who was selling Louis Vuitton purses on eBay which she did not have in stock. She collected money and looked for sellers of counterfeit LV purses priced way lower than winning bids which she bought for her buyers. After a few sales with fake fulfillment she ran out of counterfeit stock, but continued to run the auctions while sending nothing to winning bidders.

- Most fraud concerns 'phishers' who send emails telling you something is wrong with your eBay or PayPal account and urging you to sign into your account right away to check your status and stop yourself being expelled by either or both companies. We've talked bogus emails many times in *eBay Confidential* – the golden rule is **NEVER TO CONNECT TO YOUR EBAY OR PAYPAL ACCOUNT** via a link in the email. Always go to either company's main site to sign in to check your status. But phishers are becoming much more professional, a lot more cunning, and even experienced eBayers are falling prey to email scams purportedly from PayPal or eBay. The latest scam invites you to 'Become an eBay PowerSeller in seconds, log into your account right away, here's the link'. Do that and fraudsters have your eBay user name and password to order goods in your name, lots of goods, after which you'll have sellers chasing you for payment and leaving you negatives and 'failure to pay' notifications. Even if you don't lose money, your eBay reputation is irreparably damaged and that's all some phishers are after; their job is to reduce competition for other unscrupulous eBay sellers. It's a dirty practice, much resembling a protection racket, and it's every honest seller's job to have perpetrators brought to justice. Do your bit by reporting emails to spoof@ebay.com and spoof@paypal.com (or .co.uk alternatives) and send information to the Boys in Blue at the Metropolitan Police Computer Crime Unit at www.met.police.co.uk/computercrime/index.htm

- **The most alarming new trend concerns identify**

fraud and it works like this: a new eBayer opens shop, sells all manner of fabulous stuff, high value items with low, low, low prices, like cars, computers, jewellery. This is an eBay resellers' delight, so many products for you to buy, so much money for you to make, but you'll end up losing money and tarnishing your reputation forever. The big giveaway is: they do not accept PayPal, but they do have their own Credit Card Facility which you can access by phoning, emailing or by going online to give credit card details. The scam is short lived, but very profitable, because the seller does not have Merchant Facilities. But he or she does now have your credit card details which can be used to buy, buy, buy for days before you, your credit card company, or even eBay are aware a problem exists. Though I have merchant facilities myself for eBay sales, I find so few people use the facility, only three of several thousand buyers this year. Moral: pay using PayPal – they offer substantial protection against fraud – or check the status of the so-called merchant facilities seller before attempting to pay. Check by sending an email asking the name of their Merchant Facilities provider and their own Merchant ID. It goes without saying that sellers too should accept PayPal payments to stimulate buyer confidence and speedier payments than where accepting just cheques and postal orders.

There are ways to prevent being a victim yourself either as a buyer for personal or business use.

• **eBay's strongest advice is 'Know Your Seller'.** You should always check sellers' Feedback Score. More than two negatives for a low volume seller (under 100 sales) should be investigated; less than 99% positive feedback for a high volume seller (several hundred sales each month) is worth checking.

• **Be careful, make sure multiple negatives are from different sources**, not just one disgruntled buyer amongst many thousands who leaves negatives for multiple orders. Recently I found someone selling postcards, and was shocked to find they had 20 negatives among 100 feedback during the current month. On further inspection I found these were the only 20 negatives the gentleman had earned over six years of eBay trading and all came from one person. I checked that individual and discovered he rated every purchase he'd ever made as negative. Good enough for me, my seller was a very genuine seller, and sadly a victim of the

Customer from Hell.

For more advice on knowing whether to trust your seller visit: http://pages.ebay.co.uk/help/buy/ia/trusting_the_seller.html

PowerSeller tips

Little things that make a lot of difference to your bottom line

Often a tiny gap exists between making decent money on eBay and earning a better than average full-time living. But you can spend your entire day just researching ideas for improving your profits and no time actually listing items to sell. Not a good idea. But it is a good idea to let us do the research for you and report back on those little things that make all the difference to how well your business develops and how quickly you become a serious seller on eBay.

Consider:

• **Don't think if an item goes unsold first time round that nobody wants it.** Many times I've had items that failed to attract even one visitor but achieved multiple bids and high profits on second or third appearance. eBay is a fast changing marketplace with new members appearing daily and many more categories to list previously unsold goods. See the next tip.

• **A more appropriate listing category might increase sales.** For example, I had some World War One stereoviews which eBay's suggestion tool considered most appropriate for listing under 'Antiques and Art > Art > Photographs > Pre-1940', where I sold some, but not many of my 200 photographs. I relisted unsold items under 'Collectables > Militaria > World War 1' and lowered the price from £4 to £3. Almost all sold, many at £3, others up to £40 each. Magic!

• **Market your most likely best sellers outside of eBay. For example**, I had a brass statue recently depicting a Greyhound, but not just any Greyhound. This one had won the revered Waterloo Cup in 1906. I listed it under Collectables > Animals > Dogs > Greyhound but visitors were few and the statue went unsold. I relisted it in the same category, but this time I wrote to editors of specialist Greyhound and Dog Racing magazines which I'm certain helped lift a simple 'Dog' statue into a much

prized Racing collectible that sold for fifty pounds. (It cost me 10p at flea market).

• **Look for anniversaries or other events which might inflate the price of your goods significantly,** and list them close to the appropriate date. For example, an early autograph I had of Fay Wray, heroine of the film King Kong, had gone unsold over two listings, until she died recently, whereupon my third listing suddenly attracted dozens of bids and a cool £20 profit.

• **Be aware that it's just as easy (some say easier) to sell to people who have money as to others on tiny budgets.** So rather than offer cheap items with tiny profit margins, go for big ticket items. You'll probably achieve fewer sales, but you won't work so hard and there'll be fewer communications to handle. Consider: computers, fine jewellery, designer clothing, original art, cars, motorbikes. But be careful and check listing fees before pressing the submit button. Some items, like cars and motorbikes cost more to list and could eat extensively from your profits. Check carefully or do as I did and promote a pair of cufflinks shaped like motorbikes under Motorbikes > Accessories, and realise later you paid £6 in that category compared to the 35p you'd have paid under 'Jewellery'.

• **Consider setting a reserve price on a low starting bid item**. The low starting price can generate early interest, but be warned, some bidders feel cheated on encountering a high reserve price on that '99p' starting price item. Nevertheless, the low starting price / reserve price combination can result in furious bidding and high realisations and guarantees you get a good price or the item goes unsold. The reserve price is never disclosed but is always fifty pounds plus.

• **Specialise!** Become an expert in one area and make fewer costly buying and selling mistakes. Experience also saves you time researching and listing items for sale. You'll also generate repeat business from regular customers who'll come to trust you and your business.

• **List, list, list!!!** And when you think you've listed enough – LIST SOME MORE! Warning: This applies to items you've already tried and tested, and not to expensive new products about which you know little or nothing.

- **Aim to have a web site outside of eBay from which to sell additional items to customers derived from eBay.** This can be done by including a leaflet or other mention with the original fulfilment package, thanking the buyer and inviting him (or her) to visit your web site for other items of interest. Consider including a voucher for a small discount on anything ordered outside of eBay. See the next tip.

- **When you have that web site**, get it listed faster in Google's search engine by including the site url in your 'About Me' page on eBay. Someone told me that Google and other search engines index eBay related pages faster than most other sites. I wasn't convinced, so I tried, and found it worked. Start by creating an 'About Me', you'll see how in your eBay account, and say something like. 'Thank you for visiting. We are suppliers of XYZ and you can learn more about us at www.oursite.com'. Bear in mind it doesn't matter if no-one ever visits your 'About Me' page, Google and other search engine spiders will visit and index your site. I follow this technique for all new web sites and find them indexed in days or weeks, never months. Warning: eBay takes a dim view of anyone giving web site addresses in their listings, or as part of an eBay ID and active links are likely to get you barred. The rule does not apply to 'About Me' pages.

- **Use counters in your eBay listings**. These are provided by eBay, free of charge, during the listing process. Counters let you see how many visits each listing gets, from which you can plan and make changes (lots of visits but no bids is a sign something is wrong in your listing; few visits and several bids normally indicates a hot product). Few visits and plentiful bids could indicate a niche market, one with fewer members but one hundred per cent responsive buyers. But your competition can also check popularity of your listings, allowing them to capitalise on your expertise and possibly poach your ideas and products. The choice to use counters or not is up to you and you can always remove them once testing is complete and you know your product's a winner.

- **Big benefits of using 'Buy It NOW'!** The vast majority of PowerSellers sell items on the BUY IT NOW principle, thereby generating constant sales for easily available items, and meaning the same listing can be used time after time, allowing poten-

tially thousands of similar items to be delivered worldwide, often via dropshipping companies. Oftentimes the PowerSeller never even sees items he or she is selling. He or she simply lists items, takes payment, then sends order details and an agreed amount of money to another company – the dropshipping company – which then sends items direct to customers. So all you do is find 100 or 1000 high selling items, list them, sell the items, take payments, fulfill orders, then press a few buttons next week to relist those items again in just a few minutes. Look at the great majority of PowerSellers and you'll see some with many, many thousands of items listed, of which just a handful of listings are auction format. (Did you really think people selling 5,000 plus items create all those listings weekly from scratch?). See the next tip.

- **When size does matter and small is usually best**. Aim to regularly list similar (tested profitability) best selling items as opposed to continuously listing one-off items (unless you have experience of those one-off items). The benefits of this repeat product business model are many and varied and include: less time spent listing items for sale; all things being equal, regular reliable profits can be expected from relisting the same products for sale every day, week or month; planning is easier for the business man or woman who knows almost exactly what will sell next week and the week after that, as well as roughly how many sales will ensue and what profits are likely; the seller can book holidays and take days off by anticipating sales, fulfilment and delivery demands; he can confidently answer most queries by simply emailing back standard replies from wherever he or she is on holiday; the business can be highly automated, primarily through the push button process and by organising automated responses to buyers and sellers; even stock levels and reordering can be made faster and more efficient by use of standard templates or signature files which save time and energy otherwise spent placing orders by post, fax, email, telephone.

- **The magic of PayPal:** I strongly recommend you use PayPal for receiving payments and for paying eBay fees. Buyers generally prefer PayPal and will actively avoid non-PayPal sellers. People can pay immediately they receive an invoice or immediately an auction ends, meaning less likelihood of the buyer forgetting to pay later. Just go to www.paypal.com

• **Sell coals to Newcastle!** Some items naturally attract more people in their country of origin, especially collectibles such as books about New York City or 'Arizona' printed souvenir china (they'll attract more interest on eBay.com), and others from Melbourne, Australia (best on eBay.com.au), and Berlin, Germany (ebay.de). In reality, really enthusiastic bidders check the entire eBay marketplace through the 'Search' facility on every eBay page, but you can never be sure, so consider your market for every new listing ('new' meaning untested items).

• **Spread your listings to maximise your audience:** You can list each item under two categories to ensure a wider target audience. Imagine you own a car that once featured in a well-known television programme, like 'All Creatures Great and Small' or 'Coronation Street'. Do you list it under 'Cars' or 'Television Memorabilia'? The seasoned eBayer might use both categories in one listing. But if it doesn't sell, you've just lost money, more than if you'd chosen just one category. Two categories can work wonders, generating lots of bids and high realisations, but is normally best used with experience. So work at getting the first category right before expanding.

• **Advice on using photographs.** It costs 15 pence to have a 'gallery' picture of your item appear alongside your product title on eBay's listings pages. Without the gallery listing, you'll still have a cost-free picture inside the listing. Many times a gallery picture is essential, especially among high competition items such as clothing, toys, cars. Not always so for one-off and most collectors' items without a picture where enthusiastic collectors will still click through. I venture to suggest that, on occasion, a listing without a picture can generate more visits, purely out of curiosity, especially with a cryptic heading, such as 'Biggest, Fattest HoneyPot on eBay', or where pictures are largely superfluous, as for instance for books, CDs, ebooks where title itself does the selling.

• **Keep careful records of successful bidders who have paid and others who haven't.** eBay provides a reminder button for your slow-paying bidders. But proceed with caution. Remember why erasers are placed on the end of pencils – because people make mistakes – and the mistake might be yours. Check, check, check everything carefully before sending

reminders and always before writing derogatory letters to bidders or reporting them to eBay. See the next tip.

• **Use Feedback carefully.** It goes without saying, don't give negative feedback to others without making thorough checks first. The other person could have suffered a bereavement, be ill, or in the middle of a two or three day power cut and that's the reason they haven't paid you! Be fair, be nice, do unto others... ....!

• **Hot Foot It for Instant Best-Sellers.** Look for hot eBay categories, where most items attract bids, preferably multiple bids. Finding these categories, and their best-selling products, is largely down to research and hard work. When you find your niche, dominate it, have more listings than others in the niche, look for products they don't have, be first with new products. Examples from my own research: keyrings, charms, metal detectors, dog jewellery.

• **Counting on Success.** Spend time researching other people's listings, especially for products you'd like to sell. The best indicator of a popular product is the number of people actually entering the listing to obtain more information. Visitor numbers can easily be checked from counters displayed at the foot of most listings. But not all eBayers use counters. Note too that low visitor numbers may still indicate a popular product, as for instance products for tiny niche markets with fewer potential buyers but greater intention to buy.

• **Look for Ideas in the Strangest of Places.** We needed pictures of our new dog design cufflinks and wanted something special, with a luxury feel. We scan most of our products by placing them directly onto the scanner bed but find the scanner lid makes an unattractive backing for most items. We needed something different, colourful, a background to emphasise the quality of these lovely gold plated items. We tried velvet pads from jewellery boxes, plain paper, hankies, nothing worked. Then we tried M & S silk lilac undies, they worked a treat. The lilac looked wonderful against the gold and the silk wrapped delicately around the cufflinks without creasing. Better still, using that background for all of our jewellery lets regular customers spot ours among thousands of competing listings.

- **Strange Bedfellows.** Following on from the last tip, we find the scanner produces far better pictures than a digital camera, albeit some items are too big or heavy and might damage our delicate equipment. Use it for smaller, lighter items and place them gently onto the bed to avoid scratching the surface. DO NOT SCAN POINTED ITEMS OR OTHERS WITH SHARP EDGES – that is a definite shortcut to disaster.

- **Don't write or price directly and indelibly onto delicate items.** For example, write in ink on a stamp or book, append a price label onto a second hand toy, tie a tag onto a delicate necklace, and value drops drastically.

- **Do keep items as close to original state as possible.** For example, leave toys in boxes, book with dustcovers, sets of postcards in original envelopes, records in original sleeves.

- **Do repair what you can without spoiling the item or reducing its value.** Toys, jewellery and most household goods can be cleaned, clothing can be repaired or refashioned, marks can be removed from some pictures and prints. For rare items like paintings, postcards, stamps, consult an expert or leave it alone.

- **Do consider if something can be done to an item to increase perceived value and price and interest a wider audience.** Prints from early magazines can be removed, cleaned, coloured and framed, for example, and modern dolls and toys can be touched up and combined into multi-item offerings. Stamps are another good example of items often worth little on their own, but sorted into themes, say space travel, Disney, Elvis Presley, bagged and priced low, can attract multiple bids.

- **Do stay within the law or risk fines**, imprisonment or a possible end to your business for passing off modern goods as antique, intentionally mis-describing goods, trading in stolen items. 'Ignorance of the law' is no excuse. In most cases stolen items can be reclaimed by their real owners, while Trading Standards have wide-ranging powers to confiscate or withdraw 'iffy' items from sale. That's if eBay doesn't cut you off sooner.

- **Offer a free gift with your products.** This helps cut competition where your listed product is available from numerous sources. The gift does not have to be expensive, but it should be unique. Useful examples include: a book you've written or compiled yourself; a gift certificate for a discount on other of your products; a key ring or other small novelty created especially by or for your business.

- **Sell 'must have' items eBay sellers needed to run their business and attract regular**, repeat business. Choose products in constant need of replenishment such as packaging, craftwork materials, jewellery findings. You'll also find people contacting you to buy outside of eBay which helps keep your listing fees low.

- **At boot sales and auctions look for multiple same-product items in need of repair or renovation.** Few people want to repair items themselves so prices will invariably be low for damaged goods. Take the best parts from each item and create one or several perfect or near-perfect items to resell. We did this recently with a pair of Black American Money Boxes with movable parts. One box was dirty and paint badly damaged, with mechanical parts unaffected. The other was clean and unscratched but the moving bits were missing. With good bits from each matched and remodelled the money box made £40 pure profit.

- **Make a big thing of proving the authenticity ('provenance') of your products**, by including historical details in your listing or as a separate document to go with the product. Or do both and you'll find words used inside your listing will attract greater search engine traffic, while the separate document buyers receive will increase perceived value of your product.

- **Be warned against fantastic eBay testimonials placed for various sellers and products.** These testimonials might be fake and placed by sellers or their agents purely to induce confidence in their products which may not actually deserve the glowing accolade.

- **If a description is unclear,** be sure to check with the seller or risk buying something you do not really want. For example, 'old' postcards can in some people's eyes mean souvenirs of last year's holiday, while in purist collectors' eyes the term really means pre-1939 only. Only recently I bought 1000 'old' postcards from a major offline auction house specialising in postcards, only to find they were all less than three years old. For my purposes, not worth the paper they're printed on. But the fault was mine, as were the postcards which I was not entitled to return for refund.

- **What to do if you under-price an item**. If you make a mistake and price a product at £1 rather than £100 which someone buys before you realise your mistake, you do not have to part with the product. Under what is known as 'Invitation to Treat' the law holds that a contract is not formed when your buyer agrees to pay your price but when you actually take payment. Until you take payment the contract is still incomplete and you can withdraw your offer at any time. Some will say it isn't ethical, you could get negative feedback, but it's still good to know the law is on your side. Of course, like all legal rules and regulations, there are exceptions which you can learn more about at: http://www.sghlaw.com/it/articles/contract-online.html

- **Local Bobby Spills the Beans about Stolen Goods.** If you buy stolen goods, even innocently, they do not belong to you but remain the property of the original owner. You could lose money if goods are seized and returned to their true owner, and you could seriously damage your eBay reputation. A policeman friend says most stolen goods turn up at boot sales and outdoor flea markets and gives these tips to help you avoid being caught out:

Get a receipt for all major purchases. Ask the seller for name and contact details. Of course, moonlighting professionals and thieves will refuse, but most genuine sellers will oblige, at least proving you bought the items in good faith.

Many major boot sale organisers now insist on sellers registering on entry and providing name and contact details which are displayed on site.

Day-long police and police vehicle presence is a sign of a particularly high incidence of stolen items being offered at outdoor events.

The trouble with VAT

As your business grows you'll need to consider registering to pay VAT and to claim back Value Added Tax on stock and other business acquisitions. Currently the threshold is £58,000.

VAT is especially complicated for firms selling hundreds of different items all over the world as happens on eBay. eBayers selling thousands of items a month, all over the world, some items vatable, others not, will discover the whole thing is an administrative nightmare.

Add to this the fact that some very strange rules apply in determining when VAT is appropriate. For example, an old map on its own is not subject to VAT; add a mount or frame and it becomes 'decorative' and vatable.

I have to say, I've always found the VATman and VATwoman very helpful but I have frequently emerged from a phone call to their helpline feeling something wasn't quite right. I always check further and I always get answers from the VATman confirmed in writing.

My biggest problem came when I asked about old postcards, the vintage kind, and was told they are subject to VAT. A big surprise, because in thirty years of buying and selling old postcards I'd never encountered anyone charging VAT. I asked for their findings in writing, and got the statement that old postcards are Vatable. Still uncertain, I decided to check, and then the penny finally dropped. 'Old postcards' means different things to different people. To collectors 'old' means vintage; to the VATman it means cards that have not been written on, as their helpline later confirmed. It got worse. I asked about postcards from the very early 1900s that were in unused condition and worth potentially hundreds of pounds. Yes, my contact decided, if they can still be written on, you must charge VAT. Now what fool would write on a card worth so much simply because it hasn't been written on? I'm still waiting for the answer.

I decided the best choice for eBayers might be to reduce liability for VAT, and its inherent problems by:

(a) dealing in non-vatable items such as books (print copies only, not ebooks on CD or digital downloads, they are vatable);

(b) selling to countries outside the EC (such as the USA, Australia, Canada – still a massive market-place);

(c) continuously trading below the VAT threshold (a bit defeatist, but worth considering if book-keeping is not your forte).

For more information about VAT and how it affects your eBay business go to: http://customs.hmrc.gov.uk

Here's how eBay members who misspell their listing could help you pick up bargains and sell on for massive profits!

One of the very best places to buy stock is on eBay itself. This may sound strange, but many of eBay's most successful sellers, some turning over thousands of items each month, obtain most of their stock through eBay. Even better, I'll show you just how easy it is to pick up bargains from eBayers who misspell their listings!

I have bought lots of items from fellow eBayers, mainly wholesalers and book dealers. My best profits come from prints taken from old books and encyclopaedias. Because there's work involved in cutting out, displaying and describing prints individually, I find plenty of people with books to sell but unwilling to sell prints themselves. Good news for me.

The same goes for postcards I obtain from other eBayers who know the value of individual cards but prefer selling in bulk. I've bought jewellery in bulk lots, and CDs, and lots of other high profit items.

Let's see what's involved and how you can buy high profit items cheap without ever leaving home.

- **Some eBayers have several accounts, some for buying activities**, others strictly for selling. This is often to hide their buying sources from others sellers or to keep buyer feedback clean. Sometimes it's because they trade in various niche markets using a descriptive ID and shop name for each account. Many have just one account for all their buying and selling activities, for business and personal use. These are the easiest to study. When you find someone selling a lot of the type of products you'd like to sell, click on one of their listings and at the right side go to 'read feedback comments'. Click on feedback 'From Sellers' and you'll see exactly what your subject buys on eBay, how often, where from, at what price.

- **Note IDs of your subject's regular suppliers or add them to your favourite sellers.** Check feedback for your subject's main suppliers, look for other regular buyers, especially of multiple lots. Concentrate on resellers rather than personal buyers, check how successful these people are, what items sell best and attract highest prices.

- **Profit from other people's mistakes, such as items listed in inappropriate categories**, consequently attracting few bidders and low finishing prices. Finding these mistakes is more down to good luck and careful research than anything else but the results can be hugely profitable and available entirely to you. I spend at least one hour every day searching eBay, looking for profitable items attracting few bids. Sometimes I bid on those items, more often not, but I always earn more from that one hour than all the time spent acquiring stock outside of eBay.

- **Look regularly for last minute listings with few or no bidders in your favourite product category.** Bank holidays, late at night, very early in the morning, when something important is happening like a Royal Wedding or major sporting event, bidder turnout is often low and some amazing bargains are possible. Years ago, as a trader at flea markets and collectors' fairs, I quickly learned never to book any fair coinciding with a major football match, Wimbledon Finals, the Great North Run, Easter weekend. The reason was simple, no one showed up, the hall was empty all day. Now most of my Bank Holidays are spent snatching last minute no bid bargains on eBay, where you'll also find me during World Cup matches and other spectator events.

- **Spelling mistakes in listings restrict visitors and bidders**, especially if the product name or main feature itself is misspelled and unresponsive to keyword searches. I've lost count of the times I have found valuable items with misspellings and no one bidding but me. Today I found a listing for postcards by Muscha; elaborate designs, great condition, valuable collectors' items. There were five cards, starting price £49.00 and no bidders. Not surprising really because the artist's name is Mucha and his designs regularly fetch £100 plus – each! I've found valuable Bonzo dog ornaments worth about £50 each listed as 'Bonso' with me the only bidder. I've bought albums packed with high value postcards listed as 'pstcads', and many more things at a pittance of their true market value. See the next tip to learn how to profit quickly from other people's spelling and typing mistakes.

• **At www.fatfingers.com you can key in the correct version of an important keyword for your product and receive all the common misspellings and currently misspelled listings for your item**. I found those cards mentioned in the previous tip by keying 'Mucha' into fatfinger.com. Don't waste time bidding yet, except for listings about to end soon. Instead store the listings to your computer, scan them quickly, bid on most valuable and soon to end items first, take your time checking the rest. Save the listings by noting the web address or by clicking on 'File' on the toolbar, then on 'Save As', choose 'Web Page' or 'html' and store the file on your desktop. Move in fast, bid before the auction ends and sellers relist unsold items, with or without spelling mistakes.

• **A major source of misspellings is template listed items**, where you can expect that one misspelled item is followed by numerous others from the same unsuspecting seller. Sellers using *Turbo Lister* are also inclined to upload previously created templates with misspellings and other listing mistakes. Today I found someone offering 24 sets of wonderful vintage cufflinks, spelled in her case 'cuffflinks' – 3 Fs. Her starting price was low, profit potential was huge, and no one was bidding. Should I or shouldn't I? Actually I didn't, but I told her about the mistake.

• **Be careful, learn from other people's mistakes**, check your listings thoroughly for spelling mistakes and typos, look for newer or different categories for your regular products. For *Turbo Lister* be sure to download updates every few days or miss out on

better categories for your products, more attractive free templates* , and other changes to eBay listing policies.

• **Guard against your own spelling mistakes** by creating titles and descriptions in *Microsoft Word* first or other editor with spell-checking facilities. This way errors can be highlighted and corrected before uploading, unlike entries made directly into eBay or via *Turbo Lister* which lack spellcheckers.

• **eBay templates**, normally costing 7p per listing, are free using *Turbo Lister*. Download *Turbo Lister* free of charge from 'Selling Tools' inside your eBay account.

What to do when things go horribly wrong

Even the most experienced eBayers get it wrong sometimes. Let me explain with a handful of personal experiences from the past few days and show that mistakes aren't always a bad thing and most have easy solutions:

• **I uploaded a wholesale lot of dog pins, mixed breeds**, and in the listing I said, 'you get all the breeds shown in the illustration'. There are thirty breeds and, when I checked a few days later, I realised I had uploaded just one picture, of a Labrador rather than all breeds on offer. Being in a hurry with another matter I decided to let the problem listing run its course and to upload a new listing later with the correct picture of all available breeds. Three days later I sold two bundles of pins, both from the listing showing one breed only. I wrote to both buyers, explaining my mistake, and each said they bought because of the extra detail shown on that one pin which wouldn't have shown on thirty pins squashed into the same tiny space. They could see the pins were quality, and they realised that was just one item of several they'd get. The other listing, with the supposedly correct picture, closed with no sales. I say 'supposedly correct' because I now think I got it right first time; the mistake, if you can call it that, served a far greater purpose.

• **Let's say the mistake was a bad one and com-**

pletely the wrong picture or information had been listed. What should I do now? Under certain conditions, you can revise an item very easily or remove it altogether. eBay rules ban sellers from making changes or removing listings within twelve hours of auction end but only if bids have been placed. You can do little or nothing at this late stage, except contact bidders, or react later if you don't realise yet that a mistake has been made.

• **Several ways exist to remove or revise items which you'll learn about soon but for now let me tell you what I do**. Let's say I notice a major spelling mistake in my title, it looks very unprofessional and my listing won't show up when people key in the correct words to find such items. I need to correct it fast. I go to my eBay account, go to 'Selling' on the left side, then wait for the page to open. Next page shows me all my listed items, sometimes over several pages. I look for the problem item. If I know when I listed it, fine, I can narrow down the search by scrolling through auction ending times. When I find it, I click on the title and the listing opens. Next page, towards the top, there's an option allowing you to revise the item, which you click on, and wait again for the page to open. When it does, far right you'll see various options, such as 'edit title', 'edit pictures', and so on. Click on the one you want to edit, in my case the title, make the changes, scroll to the bottom of the page, click on 'submit revisions', and that's it, all done!

• **Let's say you want to end an item**. Back to the list of items you are selling, and this time instead of opening the listing, go to the 'action' menu far right, choose 'end item', and follow the pages through. You will be asked to choose a reason, such as 'Item no longer for sale', 'Item lost', and so on. Choose the most appropriate reason and close the auction. But be careful, do not ever use this option as a means of ending poor performing auctions, it's against eBay's rules to end auctions this way and too many occurrences will earn you a stern warning or even expulsion.

• **Yesterday a subscriber emailed to say an item he had bought in good faith turned out to be not as described.** He had already listed the item for sale and had bids and with less than twelve hours to go he discovered the item was a fake. He couldn't take down the listing, he couldn't revise it, what should he do? Soon you'll see the email I sent him. That email could easily be adapted to cover items you have innocently mis-described, or which have otherwise got broken or lost. Remember with more than 12 hours before the listing ends or with no bids he could have revised or removed the listing. Even at this late stage he could wait until the auction ends before confessing his mistake. I suggested the best thing was to admit the problem now, to save disappointment to the eventual winner. Here is the email which you are free to adapt any way you like to cover similar problems:

WIDGET – EBAY NO. 123456789

Hello

I am afraid I have a problem regarding the widget you are bidding on (replace 'widget' with appropriate description), item number 123456789. I bought the widget in good faith as a genuine widget but on inspection by a collector (or expert) of these items, I understand it may not be the real thing. If you are the winning bidder I am willing to send the item to you after payment for you to inspect and make your own decision. I will of course refund right away should you return the widget. But in no way do I want you to think I have offered an item knowing it was a fake. Alternatively, if you win the item we can mutually agree to close the deal without you paying and without my having to send the widget to you.

I feel rather bad about this, hence the reason I am writing to you. I very much value my business reputation and care passionately about customer service and felt I should let you know about my problem immediately I became aware of it myself.

Perhaps you would let me know what you wish me to do and I will oblige.

Best wishes

Your Name

Postage problems to stamp out fast

It's one of the most controversial areas of selling on eBay and sure to cause more disputes that anything else. It's postage.

Postage is a complex matter; it varies by delivery method, by product, by customer, by region, and it's an area the seller must make definite decisions about before ever attempting to sell.

These scenarios show how problems arise and how easily they can be resolved or prevented from happening.

- **You sent the product**, the customer claims it never arrived and reports you to eBay. It happens, all the time, for UK deliveries and worldwide, predominantly in two European countries I just hate mailing to. I can't tell you which they are, I might be called racist, but I recommend you get proof of posting for everything you send abroad. It's easy, free, and it's all eBay and PayPal need to refute a 'non receipt of product' claim. Ask your postmaster for a supply of Proof of Posting Slips, they allow about five addresses per page, and enter the details at home, before going to your post office. The postmaster checks packages against your POP (Proof of Posting) and stamps it to acknowledge those items have been received into the postal system. Keep POPs filed in date order. If anyone queries non-delivery, email them, give the receipt number, and that should be the end of it. Mention in all your listings that you always get Proof of Posting and that you are not responsible for items going astray in the post. Offer optional insurance for all deliveries at home and overseas. That mention of obtaining POP in your listing is enough to deter the most hardened eBay scoundrel who bids, pays, then reports you to eBay or PayPal and gets his money back if you can't prove it was posted.

- **Nevertheless dishonest buyers might harass you for weeks about non receipt until you give up and refund out of sheer desperation**, even if you have proof of posting. It happened to my daughter a few weeks ago. It concerned a Belgian buyer, he had 14 negatives for similar scams, and although she had proof of posting, although eBay and PayPal found in her favour, the man continued emailing abuse for several weeks. She eventually refunded him. All £4.99! I don't recommend you do the same, not necessarily, I'm just suggesting there are just times when it's best to get rid of bad pennies, even if it means losing money.

- **Mail to the United States** is the source of most non-delivery complaints. The UK postal service says post to America takes just a few days by air mail; I know it takes longer, up to a month in some cases. The best way to avoid problems is to inform American buyers that their package has been posted; give the date; give the proof of posting number, and ask them to be patient while mail is processed;

tell them their package should arrive within two weeks but not to be worried if it takes a little while longer. Other slow delivery destinations include Australia, New Zealand and sometimes Asia.

- **You work using templates or you sell the same items over and over again**. You never have to list items afresh, all items weigh the same and cost the same to post. Using templates is easy, quick, efficient – but you forgot the postage rates went up last week and you have just uploaded 100 plus items at old rates. I know how much money you stand to lose, because this scenario is no stranger to me. Sadly, in this case, you either let your problem listings run their course or revise them one by one. A tip to prevent the same mistake happening again is either to omit postage details from your listing and invoice later (not always a good idea, some people will avoid bidding altogether), or state that postage is always at cost and invite emails for specific postage costs. My own preferred method is to add a note to my listings on Turbo Lister telling me to 'CHECK POSTAGE'.

- **Weighing all your listed products separately is a major chore**, especially where you sell lots of different products of all different weights, all available worldwide, some with insurance, some going air mail, some surface. It's a nightmare, only worsened by the fact you're always holding up the queue at the post office while you weigh your stuff and struggle back home to upload it to eBay. A bit extreme perhaps although many people do work this way in their early eBay days. In time you'll realise why having a pair of postal scales at home is such a good idea. Postal scales are easily available, and relatively inexpensive, and will save you lots of time and trips to the post office to weigh items before uploading them with delivery costs included. Postal scales vary and there's something to suit all business types and size. Firms selling smaller products, like jewellery, postcards, lighters, CDs should get by with scales such as I use, which weigh items up to 1000g. They're not good for weighing computers, exercise machines, and other items that might anyway exceed the maximum weight for post office delivery. Some postal scales work in units of weight according to appropriate postage cost. They're easy to use and you can add stamps yourself before going to the post office.

- **The arrangement I have with my post office,**

which you can emulate, is that I deliver all packages to them by 3pm, they weigh and post them and telephone later to tell me how much I owe. I don't have to stand in the queue waiting to be served. Smaller packages I weigh and stamp myself.

• **Some scales outdate fast as postal rates change, such as my own which have postal prices printed on the front.** The solution is to keep the updated Post Office rates leaflet beside your scales and cross check weights against new prices. Extend the life of your scales by purchasing just as new rates are announced, not immediately before an impending rate increase. Better still buy digital scales without postal rates and have your postal rates leaflet (an up-to-date one) readily to hand.

Tips

• **Go to www.royalmail.com and click on** 'Postal Prices' currently right of home page, or click on 'Price Finder' just below 'Postal Prices' to check current prices according to destination, delivery type, weight, and other important factors.

• **Obtain a pricing leaflet from any local post office.**

• **You'll find some great offers for scales on eBay.** We keyed 'postal scales' into eBay's search box, top right of home page, and found 175 listings ranging from £4.99 at auction to £14.99 for Buy It Now digital scales. A set of 'good old commercial scales', really sturdy, and weighing much heavier items more than our tiny but reliable scales, is currently priced at £9.99 with no bidders.

• **Weigh one-off items at the end of the auction rather than weigh all individually and waste time on items that don't subsequently sell.** Inside your listing say delivery costs will be calculated after the auction and will be based on winning bidders' location and delivery preference. There is a slight problem here, in that bidders may fear you will overcharge heavily on postage as many sellers actually do. Last week I bought a pair of cufflink backings, costing £1, which cost less than 50p to post, the seller charged me £6! I won't buy from him again and I will check sellers' postage costs carefully in future before bidding. Overcome potential bidders' fears by adding something like: 'Postage and wrapping is always at cost, we do not

charge extra. If you need more information please email me before bidding.' This way, most people will bid without checking actual costs, but the option to check costs before bidding helps the tiny few who still fear a high charge after the auction. It also means you will inevitably have to weigh some items that do not sell but the number will be few compared to weighing and pricing everything before listing.

Packing Tips

• **Pack goods carefully so they don't move around in transit.** Paper and flat items should be packed in hard backed envelopes. They're relatively cheap and cost can be passed to customers as part of your postage costs.

• **Delicate items like ornaments**, glass, mirrors, should be well-covered in bubble wrap, again relatively inexpensive and can be charged to buyers.

• **Packing materials are available on eBay** at prices way below most local stationers. The reasons is, most eBayers work from home or small offices with overheads far lower than their high street counterparts. Find details at www.ebay.co.uk, under 'Business, Office & Industrial', sub-category 'Packing and Posting Supplies'.

• **Add your own name as sender on outgoing post in case delivery addresses are obliterated or the item is otherwise undeliverable in which case it will be returned to you. The same goes if the intended recipient isn't home or fails to collect the item at their** post office where, after a few days, the item will be returned to you.

• **Goods sent overseas should bear a Customs Declaration sticker** – CN 22, available from main post offices, basically stating what the item is and how much it is worth. This allows import duties to be charged at the recipient's end. Recipients are often unaware that taxes may be added and you are not obliged to tell them but it is good practice to let them know and saves you receiving poor feedback later. Even though it isn't your fault! You'll find lots of important information about sending goods abroad and receiving items from overseas at eBay's International Trading Help Board: http://forums.ebay.co.uk/forum.jspa?forumID=3004

or go to www.royalmail.com for more information.

Do you know your OOP from a WOF? How to decode eBay's auction jargon

'What does NEWOTT mean?' my eldest eBay PowerSeller daughter asked today, NEWOTT referring to the acronym 'NWOT'. I didn't know, and when I keyed NWOT into eBay's search engine I was surprised to find the acronym listed 3156 times on eBay.com.

Of course I had to find out, if only to sound professional, and sometimes to help me spot items worth buying for resale. After all, how do I know if something's worth buying if I don't know the meaning of NEWOTT or WOFF?

Those acronyms you really should know about are listed below, the rest you can learn about at: www.lasvegasvegas.com/ebaytips/acronym.php

BIN – Buy It Now
BNIB – Brand New In Box
COA – Certificate of Authenticity
FVF – Final Value Fee
NPB – Non-Paying Bidder
NW – Never Worn
NWOT – New Without Tags
NWT- New With Tags
OOP – Out of Print
PB – Paperback
PC – Poor Condition / Postcard
SH / S & H – Shipping / Shipping and Handling
WOF – Writing On Front
VG – Very Good Condition

Protecting your eBay business

I frequently get emails from readers saying their eBay accounts have been suspended for no apparent reason. Usually I think to myself the com- **plainers are being less than honest, and probably violated some eBay rules. It appears I might be wrong and many innocent eBayers are indeed having their accounts frozen at least for a while.**

Earlier this week, Terry Gibbs offered this article for our readers explaining these are really 'server errors' by eBay.

Over to Terry:

This is a quick note to help you protect yourself from a problem in eBay's system.

There is a post on the IWantCollectibles board about an eBay suspension. The problem turned out to be a "system error."

I thought this was an odd event, but over the past few weeks I have gotten emails from other readers saying their eBay accounts had been suspended for no apparent reason.

A note here. I am talking about REAL suspensions. Not the fraudulent emails we are all familiar with. These emails are DIFFERENT from the common spoof emails. They do not contain links in them, or ask for any input or response.

Spoof emails are attempts by scammers to steal your eBay account. They are designed to get you to click on a link and give a third party pretending to be eBay your account information. Real eBay suspension emails do not have links to any site within them.

All of them report difficulty dealing with eBay and then after two to four weeks of emails back and forth between eBay and suspended members, eBay sends a message like this:

"It appears that your account was suspended due to a system error that has been corrected. We apologize for the inconvenience and assure you that this unfortunate incident will not be repeated... "

However this is being repeated. Not the same accounts, but to accounts at random.

In fact, this morning I got an email from eBay telling me one of my accounts has been suspended.

Here's the email:

> Dear (EBAY USER NAME)
>
> We regret to inform you that your eBay account has been suspended due to concerns we have for the safety and integrity of the eBay community.
>
> Per the User Agreement, Section 9, we may immediately issue a warning, temporarily suspend, indefinitely suspend or terminate your membership and refuse to provide our services to you if we believe that your actions may cause financial loss or legal liability for you, our users or us. We may also take these actions if we are unable to verify or authenticate any information you provide to us.
>
> Due to the suspension of this account, please be advised you are prohibited from using eBay in any way. This includes the registering of a new account.
>
> Please note that any seller fees due to eBay will immediately become due and payable. eBay will charge any amounts you have not previously disputed to the billing method currently on file.
>
> Regards,
>
> Safeharbor Department
>
> eBay, Inc.

At this point you are probably wondering why I am telling you this.

This is a warning.

This could happen to you.

Think about it. The first person to bring this to my attention lost six weeks worth of sales. Some of the others managed to get the problem resolved in as little as two weeks. Some are still having problems after three or four weeks.

Can you afford to lose your income for two weeks or a month?

I doubt it.

I lucked out because this is not my selling account. In fact, the suspended account hasn't been used for bidding or selling in over a year. I can keep selling on my other accounts.

Do you have backup eBay accounts?

If you don't, you need to create additional accounts now. You have to have the second eBay account set up before you are suspended. I use different accounts for buying and selling. If I had 'system error' problems with a selling account, I could easily

switch my sales to a buying account.

I might lose some sales if eBay cancelled auctions as a result of the suspension, but I could quickly relist the items under a different account.

Because I already have the accounts set up and use them for buying they have feedback. They are ready to go. All I need to do to start selling on them is upgrade the buying account into a selling account by entering a credit card number.

If you still only have one eBay account, you need to create another account now. And start using it.

After you have set up a second eBay account, you should start learning other ways to protect your business. In *The Auction Revolution*, you'll learn how to create multiple streams of income. *The Auction Revolution* is a blueprint for leveraging your eBay business into a robust online business. The first half of the manual teaches you everything about eBay. The second half shows you how to remove your dependence on eBay.

You can read more about *The Auction Revolution* at: http://hop.clickbank.net/?1stinebay/nalroo

Read more of Terry's articles at www.1st-in-auctions.com

The money-multiplying secret that lies hidden in your 'About Me' page

Members are not allowed to mention or promote goods and services being sold outside of eBay. So in listings you are not allowed to include web site addresses, affiliate links, 'bricks and mortar' shop addresses. And you can't use a web address* as your eBay ID or market products direct to other eBay members via the company's communications channels.

Yet many see eBay as the tip of the iceberg, a means of pre-selling for greater profits later, a chance to cut the middleman share by back-end selling outside of eBay.

The 'About Me' page is the place to make additional sales, promote outside of eBay offers, a place to list web sites, phone numbers, email addresses, and so on. Warning: Never make it obvious you are using this page to deprive eBay of profits, 'discretion' is the keyword.

* In the early days eBay allowed use of web site addresses as IDs and have allowed continuous use to those concerned.

Ask a question, get no lies

One of the best ways to source products and make more sales is by talking to customers. Sounds obvious really but you'd be surprised how few sellers actually ask their buyers' advice about products, customer service, other people who might be interested in their products.

These ideas will help you benefit from this largely ignored market research tool:

• **Do You Want Fries With It?** Copy McDonald's who sack staff who consistently fail to offer other products customers might want to buy. For items with high postal costs, contact buyers, ask if they'd like to buy something else at a discount, no additional postage, to get the most out of their postage cost. It doesn't have to be blatant. You could, for example, send an email like this: *'Thank you for buying one of our widgets. As a valued customer I'd like to offer you ten per cent off any purchase made before your widget is shipped on Wednesday next."*

• **Ask For Customer Recommendations**. Offer some useful gift to buyers for recommending their friends and relatives to buy from you. Say something like: 'Thank you so much for your order. *If you like your product we'd appreciate you telling your friends about us and if they buy from us, ask them to mention your name and we'll send you a lovely XXX'*

• **Ask if they'd like to receive a regular ezine** or email about your range of products with lots of useful tips to help them enjoy their product or learn more about their special interest. Like this: *'Thank you for buying one of our dog kennels. We are dog lovers too and we'd love you to join our mailing list*

for lots of doggy news, you'll even get a free eBook about dog care and ways to keep your four-legged friend safe and happy for life. It normally costs £4.99 but it's free if you join our list today at www.joinushere.com'

• **Ask if there's anything you can sell for your buyers.** Buyers with a common interest, such as golfing, sewing, which happens also to be your eBay theme, might be regular suppliers for products old and new.

Introduction to eBay's new business identification system

More businesses are turning exclusively to eBay to promote their goods than are opening shop on the high street or starting out in mail order and direct mail. It's a growing trend and moves are afoot for members to be identified as business owners on eBay.

The move resembles the process in local and national newspapers where non-obvious business sellers must add 'T' for 'Trade' to their ads. This helps private individuals identify businesses from private individuals offloading unwanted household items in the classified columns.

These things are important to buyers:

• **Traders have special** legal responsibilities towards customers and there's more chance of refunds, back up support, customer support from traders than family sellers.

• **More chance of contacting business sellers** later for advice than private individuals who may lack specialist knowledge or could have moved on.

You pay your money, you take your choice and, unsurprisingly many people prefer to buy from business than private sellers.

So in the next few weeks eBay business owners can opt to identify themselves as such and increase confidence in them and the products. Members will highlight their identity on View Item pages and in Member Profiles.

Learn more about this new system by visiting eBay General Announcements at: http://www2.ebay.com/aw/marketing-uk.shtml

Stop complaints making you feel like an unpaid charity worker

Everyone gets complaints and requests for refund, it's inevitable but you do not have to lose money just because someone changes their mind about a perfectly good item. If there's a problem with the product or it was wrongly described, worse still you later discover it's a fake, then you must refund the entire amount, including postage.

Not so if the buyer just changes his or her mind.

In such a case, if the product can be restocked, these tips will stop other people's mood swings eating too deep into your profits.

Do not refund outgoing or incoming postage costs. It may be just a small amount this time, but tomorrow it could be a heavy item costing several pounds to post. If you set a precedent of refunding all postage costs you must do so on all items: light and heavy, to the UK or overseas, basic shipping rate or air mail fully insured premium rate.

Charge a restocking fee. The charge might equate to your eBay listing and final value fees where the sale can not be cancelled and fees otherwise recouped.

It's going to upset some people but frankly I don't want these people to buy from me again, and it's worth receiving unfair feedback in order to reciprocate and warn other sellers against difficult bidders.

A newcomers' guide to downloading files from the Internet

Locating the download site

Newcomers frequently experience problems actually locating the site to which they are directed to download reports. The most common reasons are:

• **Not being properly connected to the Internet,** not being connected at all, or being hampered by unusually slow data transfer speeds commonly experienced on older computers or when using dial up Internet connection. Most problems of speed, even ageing computers, are resolved using Broadband.

• **Using search engines to find the site.** Some sites are not accessible by search engine such as AOL, Google, Yahoo. This may be because companies wish to keep download sites free from search engine directories or because a site is very new and not yet recognised by search engines. Solution: Use the browser instead. The browser is normally the long empty box at the top of the screen, often prefixed 'http://www'. ISPs like AOL, Google and Yahoo have separate browser and search engine applications. If the newcomer is confused between the options he should try keying the url (web site address) into both boxes on the home page to ascertain which is the browser.

• **Failing to key in the complete and correct web site address.** Many problems result from typing errors or failure to note the address properly from download instructions. Oftentimes the newcomer fails to include essential characters like '//' in 'http://www'…. or '.html' in 'www.1st-in-auctions.com/articles.html'.

• **Ignoring case sensitivity for some web site addresses.** CasE SenSITIve means the url has some characters in upper case – CAPITALS – and others in lower case. Inaccuracies of upper and lower case characters rarely matter today for the main part of the url, that is everything between http and .co.uk (.com, .biz, or other suffix). But case sensitive sub-categories must be keyed in accurately or they will not be recognised. Examples are: www.1st-in-auctions.com/ARTICLES.html where the entire sub-category title – ARTICLES – is in upper case, or www.1st-in-auctions.com/Articles.html where just the initial letter is capitalised. In both cases you will not find the appropriate page using 'articles', 'ARTicles', or other inaccurate use of upper and lower case letters for sub-category title.

Essential software

You will rarely need special software to download files but you will require specific types to open Zipped Folders and PDF Files.

Most download sites will link to sites where you can obtain evaluation copies of *WinZip* and *Adobe Acrobat Reader*, most commonly used, respectively, for opening Zipped Folders and reading PDF Files. (Get *Acrobat Reader* at www.adobe.com and *WinZip* at www.winzip.com)

Downloading files

By far the most common downloading error concerns PDF files which can be a nightmare for novice Internet users. EXE files and other downloadable items come in a variety of designs and colours and present few downloading problems even for inexperienced users.

PDF files – saved in Adobe Acrobat format

PDF stands for 'Portable Document Format' and describes an electronic document that must be read with the *Adobe Acrobat* computer programme. The real beauty of PDF for presenting eBooks and other files is that layout remains the same for all users regardless of computer make or software programme. Compare this with *Microsoft Word*, for example, where pagination, fonts, graphics and formatting can vary dramatically between operating systems and software programmes.

Another main feature of PDF is one of creating files that can be opened and viewed on most makes of computer, even *Apple Macintosh*, unlike most EXE files which are all but useless for Mac Users.

pdcoverwhite.pdf

Next graphic shows what a PDF file looks like and how a correctly downloaded file will appear on your desktop, where the file is solitary and without Folder or WinZip. Where a PDF file is uploaded inside a Folder or saved in Zipped format the downloading process is similar to non-PDF files discussed later.

wordsells.zip

A PDF file in Zipped Folder will usually look like one of the following icons, depending on your computer's operating system. This is how a zipped folder appears on my computer with XP system:

On an older machine without XP software it looks like this:

An Internet download link looks much like this, regardless of item available for download:

DOWNLOAD HERE

The colour of the link may vary but almost certainly it will be underlined as shown above.

To download a PDF file, press your forefinger on the right side of the mouse and maintain the pressure. With right side of mouse depressed, point your cursor (arrow) at the download link (as in the last illustration) and a menu will appear looking like this:

Choose 'Save Target As' and another menu will open looking much like the following illustration and showing at the bottom of the screen that the file is in Adobe Acrobat format.

At the top of the screen at 'Save In' choose your download location and then press 'Save'.

That is it, all done!

Non-PDF files – or PDF files in folders or in 'Zipped' format

Left click with the mouse on the download link for virtually any type of folder or non-PDF file and this is the menu that appears next:

Click on 'Save' and you will see something like this:

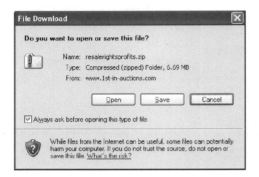

Again, at the bottom of the screen you will see you are downloading a Zipped Folder (or EXE or other) and you can choose your download location in

the same way as the PDF example. Press 'Save' and the job is done.

Common problems

- **If the 'c's are missing from the text in your pdf files** this means you are using the wrong version of *Acrobat Reader* for your computer. The correct version can be downloaded free of charge at www.adobe.com

- **If you are unable to open a zipped folder it probably means you do not have the appropriate opening software on your computer.** A free evaluation copy of *WinZip*, the most commonly used opening software, can be downloaded at www.winzip.com

- **If you have trouble opening a file or you get strange messages regarding databases or other**

applications wanting to open on your desktop, or there's a message saying your downloaded file or folder is corrupt, this usually means you have downloaded the item incorrectly from the Internet and you should attempt the download procedure again.

- **Failure to open a file or folder may also mean that you are trying to open the item using an inappropriate application**, such as attempting to open a PDF file using *Microsoft Word* when only *Acrobat Reader* will suffice.

- **If on trying to open a downloaded product you find your computer continuously tries to connect to the Internet or wants to open another programme**, this can sometimes be corrected by restarting your computer or amending your default settings. Read your computer manual or contact a more experienced user before attempting to change your own default settings or you could make the problem a whole lot worse.

- **You do not have to be connected to the Internet** to read most downloads except for those containing hyperlinks to essential online resources.